YORK NOTES

General Editors: Professor A.N. Jeffares (*University of Stirling*) & Professor Suheil Bushrui (*American University of Beirut*)

Robert Graves

GOODBYE TO ALL THAT

Notes by Christopher MacLachlan

MA PH D (EDINBURGH)
*Lecturer, Department of English,
University of St Andrews*

LONGMAN
YORK PRESS

The author is grateful for assistance with these Notes from the Imperial War Museum, the National Army Museum, the Royal Welch Fusiliers, Mr Sam Graves and many colleagues and friends, particularly Mr K. C. Fraser of the University Library, St Andrews.

YORK PRESS
Immeuble Esseily, Place Riad Solh, Beirut.

LONGMAN GROUP LIMITED
Longman House,
Burnt Mill,
Harlow,
Essex.

First published 1984
ISBN 0 582 79259 2
Printed in Hong Kong by
Wilture Printing Co Ltd.

Contents

Part 1

Introduction

The life of Robert Graves

Robert von Ranke Graves was born on 24 July 1895. The first thirty years of his life are the subject of *Goodbye to All That* and need not be described here, but towards the end of that book Graves omits certain facts. In 1926, before he left to take up his post as Professor of English Literature at the University of Cairo in Egypt, he met the American poet Laura Riding (*b*.1901). When he returned to England he left his wife and family and went to live with her. Their relationship, in which Laura was the dominant partner, was an intense and demanding one. She insisted upon Graves's complete obedience, in personal as well as in literary matters, and was capable of violent response to any sign of dis-obedience; on one occasion she jumped out of a fourth storey window (Graves, anxious to discover if she was badly hurt, leapt after her from the floor below). It was while she was recovering from this fall that Graves wrote the first version of *Goodbye to All That*, published in London in 1929.

Immediately afterwards Graves and Laura Riding left England for Majorca, an island in the Mediterranean Sea. There they set up a literary community, dedicated to furthering Laura's projects for the reform of poetry and criticism. The money for this came largely from Graves's success as a novelist. He wrote a number of mainly historical novels, including *I, Claudius* (1934) and its sequel *Claudius the God* (1934), about the Roman Emperor Claudius (AD41–54). When the Spanish Civil War drove them out of Majorca in 1936 and they had to return to England, it became evident that Graves's reputation as a writer was greater than Laura Riding's and his subservience to her appeared odd. Their relationship began to break up; by the outbreak of the Second World War in 1939 she had returned to the U.S.A. and Graves had become attached to the woman who was later to become his second wife.

This change in his life not only inspired some of Graves's best love poems but also led to his writing the book most central to his outlook, *The White Goddess* (1948). In it he states his belief in the ancient myths of Europe, which celebrate the cycle of the seasons and the fertility of the earth, presided over by a female deity; Graves regards later male-dominated religions, such as Christianity, as perversions of this true faith. Much of his poetry since then has been devoted to the goddess and her myths.

In 1947 he returned to Majorca, where he still lives. He ceased to write novels and turned to short stories, magazine articles and books about folklore and religion. These, and his poems, increased his fame, perhaps because of his delight in being provocative and unconventional. He became a popular lecturer, visiting many countries, including America, Hungary, Israel and New Zealand. In 1961 he was appointed Professor of Poetry at the University of Oxford and in 1969 he received the Queen's Medal for poetry. His latest volume of poems appeared in 1974, and *Collected Poems 1975* in the year of the title.

The First World War

The First World War lasted from 1914 to 1918 and involved all the major states of Europe, as well as the United States of America, Japan and what were then parts of the British Empire, India, Australia, New Zealand, Canada and many other colonies. About eight million people were killed and another twenty million wounded in the fighting, which took place mainly in Europe. The effects of this destruction of life were profound and nowhere more so than in Britain, which had not fought a major war since 1815 and whose people had never been engaged in a major land war. The British Army had always been a small professional one, separate from the rest of the population, but the First World War demanded far larger numbers of men, first volunteers and then conscripts. The horror and waste of the war made a deeper impression on these recruits because they had little idea what to expect. The result was revulsion not just against war itself but also against the leaders who had brought it about, organised it and insisted on its continuance to a conclusion. Those who survived the war were left with a bitter distrust of political leaders, generals and other figures of authority and a conviction that the kind of society which had allowed the war to happen was fundamentally flawed.

Goodbye to All That is valuable because it shows this historical process in detail. In the early chapters Graves describes the world before the war, the England of his childhood and schooldays. Then he describes his war experiences and shows how they changed him and turned him more and more against the outlook of his parents and their generation. Finally, he describes what life was like after the war, the terrible memory of which made it impossible to return to the old, complacent way of life. In the end he gave up the struggle and left England, its academic institutions, its class distinctions, its political prejudices and its attempts to carry on as though the war had never happened and, saying goodbye to all that, he went to Majorca, where he made a new home.

A note on the text

Goodbye to All That was first published by Jonathan Cape, London, in 1929. Graves revised it in 1957, making numerous small changes and adding a new prologue and epilogue. The revised edition was published as a paperback by Penguin Books, Harmondsworth, 1960; it has been reprinted many times. The page references in the following Notes are to the 1982 reprint.

Part 2

Summaries
of GOODBYE TO ALL THAT

A general summary

Graves begins with his earliest memories and his family background, both German and Irish. He gives an account of his early childhood and schooling and then describes his time at Charterhouse School, where he feels out of place and develops an interest in poetry. Towards the end of his schooldays he becomes friendly with George Mallory (1886–1924), the well-known Everest mountaineer, and goes climbing with him in Wales.

He leaves school in 1914. On the outbreak of war with Germany in August of that year he joins the Royal Welch Fusiliers, an infantry regiment, as an officer. After training he is sent as a replacement to the Welsh Regiment in France and experiences trench warfare near Béthune. He is re-posted to his own regiment and survives the unsuccessful battle of Loos in September 1915. In November he meets a fellow-officer, Siegfried Sassoon (1886–1967), who is also a poet. He continues to serve in the trenches, becoming increasingly war-weary. In April 1916 he returns to England on leave and is disgusted by the civilians' ignorance of the true nature of the war. He goes back to France to take part in the continuing battles on the Somme river and is wounded so severely by a shell-burst that he is reported dead. Nevertheless he recovers enough to return to the front, but the strain is too great and he is sent home as unfit. While convalescing he learns of Sassoon's protest against the war and hurries to prevent his being court-martialled. The rest of the war Graves serves in base camps in Britain.

In January 1918 Graves marries Nancy Nicholson. A year later he leaves the army. He decides to become a student at Oxford University, where he meets T. E. Lawrence (1888–1935), who encourages his literary ambitions. Graves graduates in 1925 but has no prospects, until Lawrence and others secure for him a post at Cairo University in Egypt. Graves spends a year there, frustrated by the difficulties, then resigns and comes back to England. His marriage breaks down, he becomes disenchanted with his native land and, after having written *Goodbye to All That* as a farewell to his past, he goes to live in Majorca. In an epilogue, added in 1957, Graves describes his later life. He has continued to make his home in Majorca and has been honoured by his old University.

Detailed summaries

Prologue

Graves explains his revision of the text for the second edition of 1957.

NOTES AND GLOSSARY:

grilled: (*slang*) interrogated

a suspicion of attempted murder: when Laura Riding fell out of a window (see Introduction, 'The life of Robert Graves'), the police suspected Graves had pushed her

the Depression: the prolonged economic stagnation of the 1930s

Majorca: the largest of the Spanish Balearic Islands in the western Mediterranean Sea. Graves's home is in the village of Deyá

Bartlett's *Dictionary of Familiar Quotations*: first published in 1855 by John Bartlett (1820–1905); the fifteenth edition (1980) contains four quotations by Graves

T. E. Lawrence: Thomas Edward Lawrence (1888–1935), known as Lawrence of Arabia after his legendary exploits in the war against the Turks, 1914–18. See Chapter 28

Chapter 1

Graves's earliest memories and his family background, both German and Irish.

NOTES AND GLOSSARY:

Queen Victoria's Diamond Jubilee: the celebration of sixty years' reign by the British Queen, Victoria (1819–1901)

Wimbledon: a south-western suburb of London

Shakespeare: William Shakespeare (1564–1616), the greatest dramatic poet in English literature

Sir Sidney Lee: literary critic and historian (1859–1926)

Lord Ashbourne: Edward Gibbon, first Baron Ashbourne (1837–1913), Irish lawyer

Eustace Miles: English sportsman (1868–1948)

real-tennis: the older and more complicated game, often played by royalty ('real' means 'royal'), from which modern lawn tennis is derived

Algernon Charles Swinburne: English poet (1837–1909)

Nurses' Walk: where children were taken for walks by their nurses

Wimbledon Common: a London park

Putney: a part of London near Wimbledon

Watts-Dunton: Walter Theodore Watts-Dunton (1832–1914), English writer; he cared for Swinburne when the latter's health failed

Walter Savage Landor: English poet (1775–1864); Swinburne visited him in March 1864

Dr Samuel Johnson: English poet and critic (1709–84)

Queen Anne: Queen of Great Britain from 1702 to 1714; as an anointed monarch she was reputedly able to cure scrofula (a skin disease) by touching the afflicted person. Johnson was touched by the Queen in March 1712

The Taming of the Shrew: a comedy by Shakespeare; it includes the characters Petruchio, Katherine, Hortensio and Lucio. Graves quoted the last lines of the play

Maurice Hill: Sir Maurice Hill (1862–1934), English lawyer

University Professor: see Chapter 31

Charterhouse: Graves's school; see Chapters 6–9

rugger: rugby football

the Fox sisters: Margaret Fox (1833–93) and her sister Catherine; they claimed to receive messages from the spirits of the dead in the form of knocking sounds, which they later confessed they made themselves

Marcus Aurelius: Marcus Aurelius Antoninus (AD121–180), Roman emperor and philosophical writer

Leopold von Ranke: German historian (1795–1886)

von: German for 'of'; inserted in a name it indicates noble rank

Michelet: Jules Michelet (1798–1874), French historian

Thomas Carlyle: Scottish writer (1795–1881)

Heinrich von Ranke: German doctor (1830–1909)

political disturbances of 1848: in that year there was violent protest against authoritarian government in several European states

Karl Marx: German economic and political theorist and revolutionary agitator (1818–83)

the Crimea: a peninsula in the Black Sea, scene of a war between Russia and a combined Franco-British army fighting as the allies of Turkey, 1854–6

Sevastopol: a Russian naval base in the Crimea, besieged by the French and British in the Crimean War

Tiarks: probably Johann Ludwig Tiarks (1789–1837), an astronomer who was born in Ostfriesland, on the north coast of Germany, but worked in Britain

Greenwich: the Royal Observatory at Greenwich, near London

Herr Geheimrat Ritter: (*German*) 'Mr Privy Councillor Sir'

the Kaiser: the emperor of Germany

Henry VII: King of England, 1485–1509

Milford Haven: a seaport in Wales

Colonel Graves the Roundhead: Richard Graves (?1618–?1671), cavalry soldier, who fought for both the king and the parliamentary rebels (or Roundheads) during the Civil War, 1642–51

Thame: a town near Oxford in England

Charles I: King of England 1625–49; defeated in the Civil War, he was executed by the parliamentarians

Carisbrooke Castle: on the Isle of Wight, off the south coast of England; Charles I was imprisoned there, 1647–8

Limerick: a city in the west of Ireland

Primus stove: a small paraffin-burning cooking stove, much used by campers

Protestant Bishop of Limerick: Charles Graves (1812–99), mathematician and Bishop of Limerick from 1866

Irish Brehon Laws: ancient Irish laws, codified in the eight century AD

Ogham script: an ancient British and Irish alphabet

O'Connell: no further information discovered

quiver full of arrows: an allusion to the Bible, Psalm 127:4–5: 'As arrows are in the hand of a mighty man; so are children of the youth. Happy is the man that hath his quiver full . . .'

Aberdeen: a city on the east coast of Scotland

Physician-general: a senior army doctor; John Cheyne (1777–1836) was Physician General to the Forces in Ireland, 1820–31

Sir Reginald Cheyne: Sir Reginald le Chein, great chamberlain of Scotland, 1267–9

his autobiography: published in 1930 as *To Return to All That*

Cooper's Hill: four miles west of Limerick

Cromwell: Oliver Cromwell (1599–1658), general and later leader of the anti-royalist victors of the Civil War: he invaded Ireland in 1649

Ensign: a junior infantry officer, whose duty was to carry a flag in battle

Jane Cooper: she died in 1886

Richard: Richard Graves (1715–1804), a novelist rather than a poet

Shenstone: William Shenstone (1714–63), English poet

John Thomas: John Thomas Graves (1806–70), mathematician and jurist

Sir William Rowan Hamilton: Irish mathematician and astronomer (1805–65), a friend of William Wordsworth (1770–1850), the English poet

quaternions: a higher branch of the mathematical calculus

Richard: Richard Graves (1763–1829), Dean of Ardagh in Ireland, Professor of Oratory, Greek and then Divinity in the University of Dublin

James: James Graves (1815–86), Irish archaeologist

Robert: Robert Graves (1796–1853), son of Richard Graves, Dean of Ardagh, was professor of the Irish College of Physicians; he discovered toxic goitre (Graves's Disease)

Turner: Joseph Mallord William Turner (1775–1851), English painter

Robert: Robert Perceval Graves, author of *Recollections of Wordsworth and the Lake Country*, 1869

Richard, another divine: Richard Graves (1791–1877), Irish theologian, son of Richard Graves, Dean of Ardagh

Robert, another divine: not traced; perhaps a confusion with the previous entry's brother, the doctor

Windermere: a town in the English Lake District, the region made famous by Wordsworth's poetry

British Museum Catalogue: the catalogue of the library of the British Museum, now known as the British Library, the largest library in Britain; it lists many works by the Graves family

Sir Charles Stanford: Irish composer (1852–1924)

Boosey: English music publishing firm, now Boosey and Hawkes

Bacchus: the Roman god of wine

dacently, dale: 'decently', 'deal'; the spelling is meant to imitate Irish pronunciation

Olympus: the mountain in Greece, reputed to be the dwelling place of the gods of classical Greece and Rome

a von Ranke entered a film studio: no further information discovered

one of my elder brothers: Richard Graves (1880–1960); see Chapter 31. Another elder brother was Philip Graves (1876–1953), who became a journalist; see page 243

Chapter 2

Early childhood and attitudes to religion and social class.

NOTES AND GLOSSARY:

a girl: Clarissa Graves (1892–1976)

another girl: Rosaleen Graves (*b*.1894); she became a doctor

another son: Charles Graves (1899–1971), journalist

still another son: John Graves (1903–80), civil servant and head-master

a penny: there were twelve pennies to a shilling and twenty shillings to a pound sterling

Dr Barnardo's Homes: charitable homes for destitute children, founded by Thomas John Barnardo (1845–1905)

Braille: a written alphabet for the blind in which letters are represented by raised dots read by touch; invented by Louis Braille (1809–52), a blind Frenchman

P. G. Wodehouse: Sir Pelham Grenville Wodehouse (1881–1975), English comic writer

my brother Perceval: no further information discovered

***The Globe*:**   an English newspaper

marshmallows: a kind of soft candy

a fair toff: (*slang*) 'a real gentleman'

Liberals: one of the two great political parties of nineteenth-century Britain, more inclined to reform than their opponents, the Conservatives or Tories; Liberal-Unionists were Liberals opposed to Irish separation from England

***He made them high or lowly* . . .:** from the popular hymn 'All Things Bright and Beautiful' by Mrs Cecil Frances Alexander (1818–95)

gemütlich: (*German*) comfortable

a situation in a family of ten: one involving a great deal of work for a servant

Netheravon: a small town in the county of Wiltshire in England

Baptist: belonging to a Christian sect which practises adult baptism

Wesleyans: the followers of John Wesley (1703–91), a Christian evangelist

Congregationalists: another Protestant Christian sect

Church of England: the form of Christianity recognised as the state religion in England

Roman Catholicism: the Christian Church led by the Pope of Rome

'In the Wilderness': Graves has since thought well enough of this poem to place it first in his *Collected Poems*

etc.:   in the first edition of *Goodbye to All That* Graves here included a long rambling letter begging money from him

Chapter 3

First schools, mostly unpleasant, and first sexual experiences.

NOTES AND GLOSSARY:

the Britons: a Celtic people who flourished in Britain from about 500BC to AD500; they did use a blue dye to colour their bodies, but it has nothing to do with their name

Llanbedr: a town in Wales, near the border with England

collect: a prayer; the Church of England liturgy includes set prayers for particular days

'Chevy Chase', 'Sir Andrew Barton': two traditional ballads, or folk poems in rhyming stanzas telling a story

pig-nuts: the tuber of *Bunium flexuosum*, a kind of earth-nut

Freudian: relating to the psychology of Sigmund Freud (1856–1939), who stressed the significance of childhood sexual experiences and dreams

a public school: one of the rather exclusive privately run English schools for the sons of the upper and middle classes

Rugby: a town in the Midlands of England

a secret about the headmaster: Graves is hinting that he was a pederast

'O' and 'Oh': the first is used with a following phrase and often expresses a wish or desire; the second is a detached exclamation. The distinction is pedantic and now hardly observed

Sussex: a county in the south of England

the elevens: school sports teams, cricket in summer, football in winter

Oxford: the University of Oxford, one of the oldest and most famous in England; see Chapters 23, 27 and 28

ἱσυημι, ἱημι: the ancient Greek irregular verbs 'to stand' and 'to release'

Winchester: another public school, more highly regarded than Charterhouse

Chapter 4

Childhood holidays in Germany.

NOTES AND GLOSSARY:

Munich: the capital city of Bavaria, a state in south Germany, near the Alps, mountains in Central Europe

Johannes von Ranke: German ethnologist (1836–1916)

Tegernsee: a lake twenty-five miles south of Munich
Freifrau Baronin: both these German titles mean 'baroness' in English
Aufsess: in upper Franconia, north of Nuremberg in Germany
impaled: the correct heraldic term for a shield showing half one coat of arms and half another
the Franco-Prussian War: the war of 1870–1 between France and several German states, led by Prussia
Hetchi-Petch: 'Hetschepetsch', the Bavarian dialect word for rose-hips
Greek fire: an inflammable substance used in ancient naval warfare to set fire to ships; a powerful weapon whose exact nature and use was lost in time
pretzels: crisp salty biscuits in the form of a knot
'the gipsies in the wood': from the children's rhyme: 'My mother told me I never should/Play with the gypsies in the wood'
polenta: (*Italian*) a kind of pudding or porridge made chiefly from maize flour
'*Grüss Gott, Herr Professor!*': (*German*) 'Good day, Professor!'
ex-voto: (*Latin*) 'in accordance with a vow'
burgomaster: the chief magistrate of a town (from the German 'Bürgermeister')
'love, honour, and obey': in the traditional English marriage ceremony, the bride vows to love, honour and obey her husband
Gothic characters or script: the distinctively German printed and written alphabets, not easily read by foreigners

---

Chapter 5

Growing up in Wimbledon, his mother's influence, and holidays in Wales.

NOTES AND GLOSSARY:
the end of the war: 11 November 1918
pantomimes: extravagant theatre shows, usually based on well-known fairy tales; a traditional family entertainment, especially at Christmas
Kew Gardens: the Royal Botanic Gardens near Richmond, a London suburb
Hampton Court: a royal palace on the River Thames, to the west of London
the Zoo: the Zoological Gardens in Regent's Park, London
the British Museum: in London; the largest and richest museum of antiquities in Britain, established in 1753

the Natural History Museum: a museum of plant and animal life in London

Felicia Hemans: English poet (1793–1835)

the Boer War: the war between Britain and the Boers, Dutch settlers in South Africa, 1899–1902

Fenian: the name adopted by certain Irish nationalists who tried to end English rule in Ireland by violence

Nelly: presumably a kitchen servant

Hanover: a German state

Schleswig-Holstein: a state in north Germany, on the border with Denmark

Copenhagen: the capital city of Denmark

'My son, whatever thy hand...': from the Bible, Ecclesiastes 9:10: 'Whatsoever thy hand findeth to do, do it with thy might'

'At Home' day: the day of the week when Mrs Graves would expect her friends to call on her formally

Harlech: a town on the west coast of Wales

Morfa: the Morfa Harlech, a coastal strip north-west of the town

Maes-y-garnedd: a mountain ridge east of Harlech

Gwlawllyn: Gloyw Llyn, a small lake in the mountains east of Harlech

hypocaust: the Roman heating system, using under-floor tile-covered air-ducts

Castell Tomen-y-mur: Tomen-y-mur, six miles north-east of Harlech, the site of a Roman fort, rather than villas

Artro: the Afon Artro, a small river which runs through the hills east of Harlech and enters the sea south of the town

Rhinog Fawr: a mountain peak, 2,362 feet high, south-east of Harlech

Cwmbychan Lake: Llyn Cwm Bychan, a small lake in the mountains east of Harlech

Roman Steps: a track north of Rhinog Fawr

penny-plain ... twopence-coloured: in the nineteenth century picture prints were sold in black and white for a penny or coloured by the printer for twopence

Southdown: a breed of sheep

Catullus: Gaius Valerius Catullus (*c*.84–*c*.54BC), Roman poet

the Devil's Temptation to Jesus: in the Bible, the devil tempts Jesus to throw himself from a high place to prove that God's angels will save him; Jesus refuses (see the Bible, Matthew 4, Luke 4)

George Mallory:	an English mountain climber of legendary ability (1886–1924); he disappeared while attempting to reach the summit of Mount Everest in the Himalayas
Snowdon:	the highest mountain in Wales, 3,559 feet high, and a favourite of climbers
Lliwedd precipices:	Y Lliwedd, a cliff 2,947 feet high, south east of Snowdon peak
Climbers' Club:	one of the oldest British mountaineering clubs, founded in 1898

Chapter 6

Charterhouse School: bullying and bawdy.

NOTES AND GLOSSARY:

the outbreak of war:	Britain declared war on Germany on 4 August 1914
Nevill Barbour:	English Arabic scholar (1895–1972)
St John's College:	one of the colleges of Oxford University, founded 1555
Lot ... Sodom:	in fact it is Abraham, not Lot, who in the Bible asks God not to destroy Sodom if ten good men can be found in the city (see the Bible, Genesis 18:32)
Eton:	perhaps the most famous English public school
tuck:	food, especially the kinds that schoolboys prefer
Reich:	the German Empire
Prussianism:	harsh military-style discipline and thoroughness, regarded as typical of the leading German state, Prussia
Edward VII:	King of Great Britain, 1901–10; his love of France and frequent visits there helped to improve Britain's relations with that country
entente cordiale:	(*French*) 'friendly understanding'; the phrase was applied to Franco-British co-operation against Germany before the First World War
housemaster:	the schoolmaster in charge of a school house, where the boys lived
ragging:	(*slang*) teasing and bullying
G. H. Rendall:	Gerald Henry Rendall (1851–1945), headmaster of Charterhouse, 1899–1911
early-Victorian:	belonging to the mid-nineteenth century; possibly Graves has in mind the early poetry of Alfred Tennyson (1809–92)

Chapter 7

Graves turns to poetry. The conflict between sportsmen and intellectuals at Charterhouse.

NOTES AND GLOSSARY:

The Book of Kings: there are two Books of Kings in the Old Testament of the Bible, but the incident Graves mentions occurs in the first Book of Samuel, Chapter 21; he quotes a version of verse 13

Waterloo: a London railway station, named after the battle fought against Napoleon in Belgium in 1815

Godalming: the town with the nearest railway station to Charterhouse

Guy Kendall: school teacher (1876–1960); assistant master at Charterhouse, 1902–16, headmaster of University College School, 1916–36

Raymond Rodakowski: no further information discovered

Austrian Pole: before the First World War, an independent Poland did not exist; it had been divided up by Austria, Russia and Prussia in the eighteenth century

Brooklands Racing Track: at Weybridge, near London; used for motor-racing between 1907 and 1939

Casuals: possibly a football team called Corinthian Casuals, who play friendly matches only

Korah, Dathan and Abiram: in the Bible, these three men are swallowed up, presumably by an earthquake, because they offend God (see the Bible, Numbers 16)

Founder's Court: in 1911 a statue of Thomas Sutton (1532–1611), the founder of Charterhouse, was placed in the main quadrangle

post-te: (*Latin*) 'after you'

Chapter 8

Last years at Charterhouse; boxing, the school magazine and more quarrels.

NOTES AND GLOSSARY:

Holy Ghost: the third person of the Trinity (the others are God the Father and God the Son), often represented as a dove, as in St Matthew's Gospel 3:6

gifted with tongues: able to speak many languages, a power given to Jesus's Apostles in the Bible (Acts 2:4)

Zululand: in South Africa; then a British colony

Athanasian Creed:	a statement of Christian doctrine, named after but probably dating from a century and a half later than St Athanasius (*c.* AD296–373); the quotation relates to the mystery of the Trinity, the three-in-one nature of the Christian God
broad-Church:	a group of Christians who tolerate variation of religious opinion
Cambrai:	a town in north-east France, scene of a British attack in November 1917
Dick:	identified as George Harcourt Johnstone, Baron Derwent (1898–1949)
Plato:	Greek philosopher (*c.*427–348BC); some of his works advocate homosexuality
Shakespeare:	some of his *Sonnets* (1609) express passionate friendship for a younger man
Michelangelo:	Michelangelo Buonarroti (1475–1564), Italian sculptor and architect; he wrote sonnets of love to both men and women
welter-weights:	the class of boxers weighing between 135 and 147 pounds
cherry-whisky:	perhaps whisky sweetened with cherries, or cherry brandy
a pledge card:	a written promise not to drink alcohol
Queen Anne silver:	silverware dating from the reign of Queen Anne (1702–14)
christening mugs:	small engraved silver cups commemorating infant baptism
Cambridge:	the University of Cambridge, the other old and famous English university, rival to Oxford
Shaw:	George Bernard Shaw(1856–1950), Irish playwright and political commentator, also well-known as a drama and music critic
Samuel Butler:	English novelist and controversialist (1835–1902); see page 62
Rupert Brooke:	English poet (1887–1915)
Wells:	Herbert George Wells (1866–1946), English writer, especially of science fiction
Flecker:	James Elroy Flecker (1884–1915), English poet
Masefield:	John Masefield (1878–1967), English poet and Poet Laureate, 1930–67; see also Chapter 27
Edward Marsh:	English editor and encourager of poets (1872–1953)
Mr Asquith	Herbert Asquith (1852–1928), British Prime Minister, 1908–15
Cyril Hartmann:	English historian (1896–1967)

Green Chartreuse: the name of a liqueur made by the monks of Chartreuse in France; 'Charterhouse' is in fact the English equivalent of the French 'Chartreuse'

new-bug: (*slang*) a new boy at school

hash-pro: obscure; on page 37 Graves says 'pro' meant 'scholar' at Charterhouse

Farncombe ... Weekites ... Bridge: places near Charterhouse

Charterhouse Magazine: perhaps a weapon store, rather than a periodical

stingers: (*slang*) difficult questions

the horse that rolls Under Green: the horse that pulls the grass roller on one of the school playing fields

colours: badges awarded to permanent members of school sports teams

cocked-up for festivity: punished for jocularity (?)

'cube': cubicle or room

Frank Fletcher: Sir Frank Fletcher (1870–1954), headmaster of Charterhouse, 1911–35

an 'I told you so': an occasion for smug reminders of past unheeded warnings

classical exhibition: a prize of money to be used to pay for studying the classics at university; see page 239

Anthony Wilding: a New Zealander (1883–1915), four times All-England tennis singles champion, killed in France in the war

Judas Iscariot: the disciple who betrayed Jesus

Governing Body: the governors of the school, responsible for its finances and teaching appointments

preparation: the boarding school equivalent of homework

a fag: a schoolboy servant; senior public schoolboys are often allowed the services of a younger boy

Empire Service League: the National Service League, founded in 1901; Earl Roberts was its president from 1905

Earl Roberts of Kandahar: Frederick Roberts, V.C. (1832–1914), who was made an earl in 1902; soldier and general

V.C.: Victoria Cross, the highest decoration for bravery awarded to British servicemen, instituted in 1856

Officers' Training Corps: a military training body for schoolboys; it had units at most public schools in Britain

Sir William Robertson: English soldier (1860–1933); Chief of the Imperial General Staff, 1915–18

'Fuzzy' McNair: Captain Eric Archibald McNair (1894–1918), Royal Sussex Regiment; he won his V.C. in 1917

Sturgess: no further information discovered

Honourable Desmond O'Brien: no further information discovered

Bruges: a town in Belgium, captured by the Germans, October 1914

Royal Flying Corps: the air warfare unit of the British Army, created in 1912 and joined with the Royal Naval Air Service to form the Royal Air Force in 1918

the Western Front: the war theatre in France and Belgium, where French, British and other forces faced the Germans; the Eastern Front lay in what is now Poland, where Russia faced Germany and Austria-Hungary

A. G. Bower: he played five times for England between 1924 and 1927 in cricket Test matches

Woolf Barnato: English sportsman (1895–1948), best known as a racing driver between the wars

Richard Hughes: English novelist (1900–76)

Richard Goolden: English actor (1895–1981)

Vincent Seligman: English author (*b.*1896)

Venizelos: Eleutherios Venizelos (1864–1936), Greek politician

the *Daily Mail*: a British national newspaper

Chapter 9

Climbing in Wales, with George Mallory and others.

NOTES AND GLOSSARY:

Quellyn Lake: Llyn Cwellyn, to the west of Snowdon

Carlsbad plums: candied plums

Geoffrey Keynes: English critic (1887–1982), editor of the writings of the English poet and painter William Blake (1757–1827)

gunner: artilleryman

Irvine: Andrew Comyn Irvine (1902–24), the climber who disappeared with Mallory on Mount Everest

James Boswell: Scottish writer and biographer (1740–95)

'How mine enemies flee . . .': this imitates the English of the Authorised Version of the Bible, 1611, but is not a direct quotation

Workers' Educational Association: founded in 1903 to promote adult education, especially among the working class

H. E. L. Porter: Harold Porter (1888–1973), famous as a mountain-climber, especially in New Zealand

Kitty O'Brien: Kate O'Brien (1897–1974), Irish novelist and dramatist

Conor O'Brien: Edward Conor Marshal O'Brien (1880–1952), Irish yachtsman and author

Geoffrey Young:	English mountaineer (1876–1958)
a Red Cross unit:	an ambulance unit
Champéry:	in the Swiss Alps south of Lake Geneva
Morgins:	a small town north of Champéry
Crib-y-ddysgel:	a 3,493-foot high subsidiary peak of Snowdon
scree:	loose stones
Robert Trevelyan:	English poet and translator (1872–1951)
Crib Goch:	a 3,023-foot high subsidiary peak of Snowdon

Chapter 10

The outbreak of war, 1914; Graves joins the army.

NOTES AND GLOSSARY:

the regular forces:	the full-time, professional army and navy
violation of Belgian neutrality:	the German army tried to outflank the defences of France by advancing through the small neutral state of Belgium in August 1914; this provoked Britain's declaration of war on Germany
Antwerp:	a major port in Belgium, not captured by the Germans until October 1914
Kölnische Zeitung:	a newspaper published in Cologne in Germany
Le Matin:	a French newspaper
The Times:	the London newspaper
Corriere della Sera:	an Italian newspaper
a company:	an infantry formation; there were four companies in a British battalion
mess:	the collective dining arrangements of soldiers, and hence the men so grouped together, usually by rank or formation
Alexandra Palace:	a large building in north London, completed in 1878; during the war it was used to house refugees and then as an internment camp for enemy citizens
Dick Poore:	Admiral Sir Richard Poore (1853–1930), Commander-in-Chief at the Nore, 1911–15; he married Ida, daughter of Charles Graves, Bishop of Limerick (see page 13)
the Nore:	a naval anchorage at the mouth of the river Thames
Zürich:	a city in Switzerland
'Pour le mérite':	(*French*) 'for merit'; the name of the highest German decoration for bravery, established in 1667 and given only to officers. It was awarded 687 times in the First World War (and never since); the V.C., which can be won by all ranks, was awarded 633 times

Bolsheviks:	the revolutionary party, led by V. I. Lenin (1870–1924), which seized power in Russia in 1917
Rheims:	a city in northern France, east of Paris
Lutheran:	a Protestant Christian of the church founded by the German reformer Martin Luther (1483–1546)

taking a commission instead of enlisting: becoming an officer rather than an unranked soldier (or 'private')

Royal Welch Fusiliers: see the next chapter for further details about this regiment

Wrexham:	a town in north-east Wales
adjutant:	the officer who deals with regimental administration
C. L. Graves:	Charles L. Graves (1856–1944), assistant editor of the humorous magazine *Punch*, 1928–36, and contributor to another magazine, *The Spectator*
a sovereign:	a gold coin, worth one pound sterling

Samuel Butler's *Note Books*: published in 1912

The Way of All Flesh: published in 1903, Butler's autobiographical novel described his rejection of his father's Christianity

the two *Erewhons*: Butler's novels *Erewhon* (1872) and *Erewhon Revisited* (1901), set in an imaginary land, satirise Victorian customs and institutions

Royal Military College at Sandhurst: founded in 1802 as a training school for regular army officers, Sandhurst is in Kent, south-east of London

militia:	volunteer part-time forces based in Great Britain
the Square:	the parade ground
mufti:	civilian dress, as opposed to military uniform
talking shop:	discussing military matters
platoon:	about fifty men, divided into four sections; there were four platoons in a company
Burma, 1885:	British troops invaded Burma from India in 1885
'Rooti':	from a Hindustani word meaning bread; the long-service medal was not perhaps regarded as a rarity

a Kipling character: Rudyard Kipling (1856–1936) wrote many stories about British soldiers in India

Quetta:	now a city in Pakistan

North-West Frontier: the border between British India and Afghanistan, a troubled corner of the British Empire

the British Consul in Jerusalem: the representative of the British government in that city in what was then Palestine

Lancaster:	a town in the north of England
Liverpool:	a major port on the west coast of England
German band:	itinerant groups of German musicians were a feature of pre-war life in Britain

our voluntary system: to begin with, the British army and navy were recruited from volunteers only; not until January 1916 was conscription introduced

In the summer of 1915, *The Times* reprinted . . .: an exhaustive search through *The Times* of 1915 failed to discover this article

Manchester: a city in the English Midlands, near Liverpool

frogged: decorated with loops of braid

the border counties: on the border between England and Wales

a training camp holiday: as Special Reservists (or militia), the men would only be required in peacetime to serve two weeks in a military camp, usually in summer; but the war extended their service indefinitely

'Halt! Who goes there?': the traditional British Army challenge made by a sentry to anyone approaching

live rounds: real bullets, capable of killing

the chops: (*slang*) the jaw

Chester: a town in England, near the Welsh border; the main town of the county of Cheshire

Crawshay: C. H. R. Crawshay (1882–1937), later promoted to Lieutenant-Colonel; see Chapter 19

a soldier-servant: every officer had a soldier who looked after his equipment

the Orderly Room: the administrative office of an army unit

the Grand National: a horse race held annually over the course at Aintree, near Liverpool

Orderly Officer: the officer on duty in the Orderly Room

Johnny Basham: Sergeant John Basham became welterweight champion of Great Britain on 10 May 1915; his opponent was not called Boswell

Lonsdale Belt: a decorated belt awarded to British boxing champions, a practice begun in 1909 by the Earl of Lonsdale (1857–1944)

M.P.: Member of Parliament

W. G. Gladstone: William Glynne Charles Gladstone (1885–1915), whose home was Hawarden Castle, Cheshire; he was a grandson of William Ewart Gladstone (1809–98), several times British Prime Minister

Lord-Lieutenant: chief magistrate of a county in Britain

second-lieutenant: the lowest officer rank in the army

War Office: the Government ministry for the army, located in London

General French: Sir John French (1852–1925) later Field Marshal, commander of the British army in France, 1914–15

dear him!:   a facetious third-person rendering of the exclamation 'Dear me!'

Dalkey: a town on the east coast of Ireland, just south of Dublin

Trinity College, Dublin: the leading Irish university, founded in 1591

all the other Williamses: surnames such as Jones, Davies, Rees and Williams, are very common among the Welsh, so distinguishing nicknames are frequently used

Private: the lowest rank in the British Army

Anglesey: an island off the north-west coast of Wales

colonel: the officer who commands a battalion

khaki: the brownish-yellow colour adopted, instead of red, for British Army combat uniforms in the late nineteenth century (from an Urdu word meaning 'dusty')

Cock Robin: the British bird called a robin (*Erithacus rubecula*) has bright red breast feathers

'*Danger on the line*': like a red warning sign on a railway line

Festubert: in northern France, near Neuve-Chapelle; scene of a British attack, 15–27 May 1915

Loos: in northern France, north of Arras; scene of a British attack, 21 September–13 October 1915 (see Chapter 15)

King's Regulations: the code of rules applied in the army

non-commissioned officer: one belonging to the lower army ranks, above private but below full officers, for example, corporal, sergeant, sergeant-major; often abbreviated to N.C.O.

Lights Out: at the end of the day, when the troops go to bed

99 Davies: this Davies is identified by the last two digits of his army number

as you were: return to what you were doing before; that is, cap on

Pte: private

hacting horderly sar'nt: acting orderly sergeant (the spelling imitates pronunciation)

haad ... baad: had, bad (here spoken with a long Welsh vowel sound)

the four stock words: probably 'bastard', 'bloody', 'bugger' and 'fuck'; Graves uses or hints at them all in *Goodbye to All That*

tole ... wass ... axed: told, was, asked (imitating Welsh accent)

effing c———: (*obscene*) fucking cunt

Hindenburg Line: a major German trench fortification, named by the Allies after the German commander, Field Marshal

Paul von Hindenburg (1847–1934); the Germans called it the Siegfried Line (after a legendary German hero). It ran from near Arras in the north to near Soissons in the south and was breached by the British in October 1918

Liverpool Exchange Station: a railway station in Liverpool

Arras: a town in northern France, behind the British lines

regimental goat-major: the soldier who tends the goat which is the traditional mascot of the Royal Welch Fusiliers

lese majesty: high treason

Colonel-in-Chief: the ceremonial head of the regiment; royal regiments have the monarch as colonel-in-chief

Windsor: near London; the castle there is a royal palace

reduced . . . to the ranks: made him a private

chapels: the extreme Protestant Christian sects in Wales called their meeting-places chapels rather than churches

Merioneth: a county of north Wales

Lloyd George: David Lloyd George (1863–1945), Welsh politician and British Prime Minister from 1916 to 1922; see page 168

Boer War field-tactics: Graves implies that the Army's fighting methods were nearly twenty years out of date

section: the smallest army formation, consisting of an officer or N.C.O. and about ten men

the retreat from Mons: on arriving in France in 1914, the British had advanced to Mons in Belgium, but had been forced to fall back before the German advance

skrimshanking: (*slang*) shirking hardships or duty

Chapter 11

The Royal Welch Fusiliers; traditions, customs and war service.

NOTES AND GLOSSARY:

senior in the line: before 1881, each British infantry regiment had a number which showed its place in the order of battle of the army; the lower the number, the higher the status or seniority of the regiment. Though no longer used, these numbers and their meaning are still remembered by the regiments

battle-honours: regiments which took part in a battle were allowed to put its name on their flags (called 'colours')

none more recent than the year 1711: before 1914, the Bedfordshire

	Regiment had eight battle-honours, the first five in common with the Royal Welch Fusiliers
Tommy:	short for 'Thomas Atkins', the traditional name for a British soldier because used as an example in specimens of official forms since 1815; the Duke of Wellington (1769–1852) is said to have inserted this name and described Thomas Atkins as of the Twenty-third Foot
broken square:	at the battle of Quatre Bras in Belgium, 1815, the second battalion of the Black Watch, although in defensive square formation, suffered heavily when attacked by French lancers
1888 combinations:	in 1881 (not 1888) the British infantry was reorganised; many separately numbered battalions were paired to form two-battalion regiments
no casualties:	at the battles of Vimiero and Rolica in Portugal in 1808, the 91st Foot (later the Argyll and Sutherland Highlanders) were in reserve and suffered no casualties, though they received the battle honours
The Boyne … Aughrim:	battles fought in Ireland, in 1690 and 1691, against Irish Roman Catholic rebels
the capture of Lille:	the successful seige of Lille, in northern France, 1708
Sir John Fortescue:	English military historian (1859–1933), author of a thirteen-volume *History of the British Army* (1899–1930)
Malplaquet, Albuhera, Waterloo, and Inkerman:	battles fought in France, 1709, Spain, 1811, Belgium, 1815, and the Crimea, 1854; all were victories over the French, except the last, which was over the Russians
Minden:	fought in north Germany, 1759; again a victory over the French, in which the British infantry, while not exactly charging the French cavalry, did attack it and repel its charges
York Town:	on the eastern coast of North America, where in 1781 a British army surrendered to French and United States forces
the full honours of war:	they were allowed to march out to surrender with flags flying and bands playing, and carrying their weapons
Lexington … Guildford Court House … Bunker Hill:	battles of the American War of Independence, fought in 1775, 1781 and 1775
Redan Redoubt:	a major feature of the defences of Sevastopol, besieged during the Crimean War, 1854–56

Scutari: a Turkish port on the Bosporus, now known as Uskudar; a British base in the Crimean War

Balaclava helmet: a cloth or woollen one-piece headcovering, which leaves only the face exposed; named after the small harbour used by the British besiegers of Sevastopol

the effects: the personal possessions

Sir Luke O'Connor: Major-General Sir Luke O'Connor, V.C. (1832–1915); he became colonel-in-chief of the Royal Welch Fusiliers in 1914

queue: pig-tail or single plait of hair, the accepted hair-style of eighteenth-century Europe, retained by the British Army long after it had gone out of civilian fashion

William IV: King of Great Britain, 1830–7

Napoleonic Wars: the wars fought between 1805 and 1815 against Napoleon Bonaparte (1769–1821), Emperor of France

Guards . . . Line: certain British regiments, both cavalry and infantry, are designated royal guards and traditionally attend the sovereign; the other regiments took their allotted places in the battle-line

warrant-officers: highest rank of non-commissioned officers

Corunna: in 1809 a British force in Spain retreated to the northern port of Corunna and escaped by sea from their French pursuers

Military Cross: an award for bravery given to army officers

Buckingham Palace: the chief royal residence in London since the nineteenth century

King George: George V, King of Great Britain, 1910–36

Daily Herald: a newspaper founded in 1912 and dedicated to a socialist point of view

'Strewth!':   (*an oath*) 'God's truth!'

Egypt: the British reconquered Egypt in 1801, after Napoleon had abandoned his troops there

Henry Tudor: Henry VII, King of England, 1485–1509; his grandfather was Welsh

Owen Glendower: a Welsh nobleman (?1359–?1416) who resisted English domination of his country

Lord Herbert of Cherbury: philosopher, poet, diplomat and soldier (1583–1648); Cherbury, or Chirbury, is in Shropshire, an English county bordering Wales

New Army: the many new battalions formed from volunteers in 1915; they were looked down upon by the older regular battalions

Yorkshire: a county in the north of England

the Peninsular War: the war fought to drive the French from Spain and Portugal, 1807–14

St David's Night: the evening of 1 March; St David (sixth century) is the patron saint of Wales

leeks: a traditional Welsh symbol

the Summer Palace at Peking: looted after a punitive expedition to the Chinese capital by a multi-national force in 1900

despite Shakespeare: in his play *Henry V* (1598–9), Act V Scene 1, Shakespeare has a Welsh character force an Englishman to eat a leek as a mark of respect to Wales

Major Toby Purcell: Tobias Purcell (*d.*1692) became colonel of the Royal Welch Fusiliers in 1691; he fought at the Boyne, 1690, as a major and the spurs he wore were kept by the regiment until lost in Canada around 1840, either in a fire or in a lake, though they are still honoured by a regimental toast

Newfoundland: an eastern province of Canada

Shenkin ap Morgan: a legendary Welsh landowner, subject of an ancient ballad, whose virtues are expanded upon in a traditional Royal Welch Fusiliers toast

***The British Grenadiers*:** a traditional marching song dating from the eighteenth century; the exact origin of its words and music is unknown. See also page 230

to Palestine: to serve in the war against the Turks

Gallipoli: in 1915 Britain and France tried to seize from the Turks the sea passage from the Mediterranean Sea to the Black Sea (and hence to their ally Russia) by landing troops on the Gallipoli peninsula at several points, including Suvla Bay; the result was a costly failure

Gaza: a town in what was then Palestine, scene of three battles between British and Turkish forces in 1917

Givenchy: a town in northern France, five miles east of Béthune, attacked by the Germans in January 1915 and the scene of much fighting later (see Chapter 19)

the brigade: the brigade of foot-guards

orders: awards or medals

only three exceptions: one of these must be Siegfried Sassoon (see Chapter 16, page 146), who was awarded the Military Cross in June 1916

British Expeditionary Force: the title of the British army sent to France in 1914; often abbreviated to B.E.F.

first battle of Ypres: fought in November 1914; two more battles were fought near this Belgian town, in 1915 (when the Germans used poison gas for the first time) and 1917

Bois Grenier: in northern France, five miles south of Armentières

Aubers Ridge: in northern France, between Béthune and Lille; scene of a British attack in May 1915

Fricourt: in northern France; a British objective in the Somme offensive of July 1916

the Quadrangle: a German trench north of Fricourt, taken by the British on 5 July 1916 in the Somme offensive; see page 174

High Wood: another Somme attack objective, taken 15 September 1916; Graves was wounded near here (see Chapter 20)

Delville Wood: not far from High Wood and also the scene of bitter fighting, July 1916

Ginchy: a town near Delville Wood, taken by the British, 3 September 1916

the Somme: the Somme river area in northern France was the scene of a series of British attacks in the second half of 1916, with many casualties and small gains; see Chapter 20

Puisieux: a town west of Bapaume in northern France, captured by the British, 26 February 1917

Bullecourt: a town in northern France south-east of Arras, in the Hindenburg Line, attacked by the British in April and May, 1917

the Armistice: the cessation of fighting, 11 November 1918

the Battle of the Pyramids: part of Napoleon's conquest of Egypt, 1798

Chapter 12

Graves arrives in France and goes into the front line with the Welsh Regiment.

NOTES AND GLOSSARY:

Harfleur: a small town on the north coast of France

Le Havre: a port on the north coast of France

fatigues: the army term for physical labour

jig-a-jig: fornication

'up the line': from the base camp to the fighting trenches

quartermaster: the senior N.C.O. in charge of stores and supplies

time-serving N.C.O.'s: professional soldiers who had joined the army before the war to serve a fixed number of years

Richebourg:	in northern France, near Festubert; the fighting here was part of the battle for Aubers Ridge, 1915
Rue du Bois:	near Richebourg and also involved in the Aubers Ridge attack
Cardiff:	the capital city of Wales
Lee-Metford:	a military rifle, used by the British Army from 1888 to 1895; it did have a safety catch, although its predecessor, the Martini-Henry, adopted in 1872, did not
Egypt in 1882:	the British occupied Egypt in 1882 after winning the battle of Tel-el-Kebir
Béthune:	a town in northern France, about 100 miles north of Paris, and behind the British lines
Saint Omer:	a town in northern France, between Béthune and the English Channel
nap:	a simple card game
francs:	the franc is the unit of French currency
Cambrin:	a French village east of Béthune, just behind the British line
Aberystwyth:	a hymn tune by Joseph Parry (1841–1903), named after a Welsh town
column of fours:	soldiers marching four abreast, the standard formation on long marches
in the pink:	(*slang*) in the best of health
fags:	(*slang*) cigarettes
booger:	(*a swear-word*) bugger
respirators:	the First World War term for a gas-mask
field-dressings:	emergency bandages for use in battle
jam-tin bomb:	a bomb made by packing explosive into a used jam-tin
Lewis or Stokes guns:	the Lewis machine gun was developed before the war, but widely adopted by the British Army only in 1915; it was lighter and more portable than other types. The Stokes 3-inch mortar was invented by Wilfred Stokes in January 1915
mate:	(*slang*) friend
to do my bit:	(*slang*) make my contribution to the war-effort
local armistice:	surprisingly common in the trenches, where both sides often agreed to live and let live; see the first paragraph of Chapter 14
D.C.M.:	Distinguished Conduct Medal, an award for bravery given to soldiers below officer rank
the last show:	the last battle or military action
a dud show:	(*slang*) a defeat or military failure

Dai:	a common Welsh forename, equivalent to English 'David'
a Fritz:	a common German name, here applied to any German soldier
No Man's Land:	the area between the opposing trenches, controlled by neither side
'Deoul!':	Graves's spelling of the Welsh word 'diawl' meaning 'devil'
f———ing:	fucking
put paid to:	(*slang*) fatally wounded
dressing-station:	first-aid post
'Christmas-tree':	because it resembled the trees hung with ornaments which decorate British homes at Christmas (25 December)
got it:	(*slang*) been killed
war-babies:	children fathered by soldiers outside wedlock; the implication is that there is great sexual licence in England
fire-steps:	raised ledges upon which the soldiers stood to fire out of the trenches
traverses:	right-angled indentations in the trench-line to prevent the enemy firing straight along it
communication trenches:	trenches joining the front-line fighting trenches with the supporting trench lines behind them; in theory, all movement to and from the front line was supposed to be made below ground level along trenches
the limit:	(*slang*) the end, as far as things can go
scuppered:	(*slang*) killed
unmasked:	undisguised
got the wind up:	(*slang*) become nervously excited or frightened

do and die ... reason why:	an allusion to Tennyson's poem 'The Charge of the Light Brigade' (1854), lines 14–15:
	    Their's not to reason why,
	    Their's but to do and die ...

Stand-to:	short for 'stand to arms', the order to take up battle positions in expectation of an attack, which often came in the half-light of dawn or dusk
R.E.:	Royal Engineers, the Army unit expert in fortifications and building work
a doss:	(*slang*) a sleep
ball:	bullets, rather than harmless blank cartridges
Maxim:	a type of machine gun, named after its American inventor, Hiram Maxim (1840–1916)

foresight:	the aiming indicator on the muzzle of a rifle
whizz-bangs:	an onomatopoeic term for mortar bombs
sap:	a small trench dug from the main front line out towards the enemy's position
the last push:	the last offensive
Auchy...Huisnes... La Bassée:	villages in northern France east of Béthune and north of Loos
a fixed rifle:	a rifle mounted in position to fire at a predetermined target; in Chapter 16 Graves describes their use
Bavarian Guards Reserve:	the German Army was really an amalgam of the armies of the states which had united to form Germany in 1870 and the regiments retained their old titles and status
Sights at four hundred:	rifle sights set to fire at a target 400 yards away
Rugby:	an English public school
Clare, Cambridge:	Clare College (founded 1326), one of the colleges of Cambridge University
'Silent Night':	ironically, the title of a Christmas carol written and composed by an Austrian priest, Joseph Mohr (1792–1848)

Chapter 13

Extracts from letters, May and June 1915; trench-fighting near Béthune.

NOTES AND GLOSSARY:

La Bourse:	a village south of Béthune
pavé:	(*French*) paved or cobbled; that is, a main road
Housewife:	a small case holding needles and thread
Disc, identity:	each soldier wore a disc stamped with his army number to show who he was if he was killed
spine protector:	a cloth pad worn in the small of the back to counter the effects of heat
Rolls-Royce:	a make of motor-car
the staff:	the officers in headquarters behind the lines who plan and direct the operations actually carried out by the front-line troops
Monsieur:	(*French*) 'Mister'
Souchez:	a town north of Arras where the French mounted an offensive in May 1915
Notre Dame de Lorette:	high ground near Souchez
C.O.:	Commanding Officer
shrapnel:	a shell packed with bullets which sprayed out when it exploded; named after its British inventor, Henry Shrapnell (1761–1842)

Vermelles les Noyelles: a town a mile or so south of Cambrin, near Béthune

Salvation Army: a Christian missionary and charitable organisation formed on military lines by William Booth (1829–1912) in 1878

Mentioned in dispatches: referred to by name in the official report of a military operation; the next best distinction to winning a medal

pinching: (*slang*) stealing

on the peg: (*army slang*) on a disciplinary charge

Wash me in the water . . .: this and the next line are alluded to by T. S. Eliot (1888–1965) in his poem *The Waste Land* (1922), lines 199–200

'cushy': comfortable or fortunate; here it refers to a wound which is neither fatal nor crippling but will require a prolonged hospital leave in Britain

'Blitey': usually spelt 'Blighty'; from a Hindu word meaning 'foreign', especially 'European', and hence used by British soldiers in India to mean England or home

bloke: (*slang*) man

a square-head: a German soldier, because of his close military haircut

Finee: (*slang*) finished

boutillery: bottle-factory (from the French 'boutillerie')

bonny: (*Scots*) beautiful

na: (*Scots*) not

transport men: soldiers who look after the battalion horses and waggons behind the lines

Haking: General Sir Richard Haking (1862–1945), who commanded the First Division, 1914–15

morale: (*French*) 'fighting spirit'

Cuinchy brick stacks: a mile or so north-east of Cambrin

rifle-grenades: grenades fired from specially adapted rifles and hence travelling further than hand-thrown ones

sausage mortar-bomb: presumably a large and fearsome projectile of elongated shape

Petticoat Lane . . . Lowndes Square: London street names here applied to parts of the British trench system

'Put it there': 'put your hand in mine', an invitation to shake hands

a letter to censor: officers had to read through their soldiers' letters home and remove passages revealing military information

sleep with: have sexual intercourse with

'gaffs':	(*slang*) entertainments
Town Major:	officer in charge of the town as a military base
Poimbert:	a French town in German hands, location uncertain
salient:	a forward bulge in the front line, vulnerable to enemy fire from either side as well as from in front
'The Farmer's Boy':	an English folk song
the mine:	explosives lodged at the end of a tunnel dug under an enemy position
C.S.M.:	Company Sergeant Major (misprinted as 'C.M.S.' in the Penguin edition)
versus:	(*Latin*) 'against'
Skelton:	John Skelton (?1460–1529), English poet; Graves quotes from his poem 'Speak Parrot' (?1521) lines 214ff
mannes:	man's
popajay:	in modern English 'popinjay', a parrot
coup de grâce:	(*French*) 'the final blow'
Norman:	dating back to the time of the Dukes of Normandy (about AD900–1100)
St Peter:	Simon Peter, one of Jesus's disciples, martyred at Rome about AD64; traditionally, he keeps the gate of heaven and is always pictured holding the keys
skipper:	the captain of a small ship; often used, as here, to address a leader
half-a-crown:	a coin worth two shillings and sixpence, half the value of a crown, worth five shillings
civvies:	(*slang*) civilian dress
undetonated:	without the detonator needed to explode it
cockney:	pertaining to the working class of London

Chapter 14

Further trench experiences; Graves is posted back to the Royal Welch Fusiliers.

NOTES AND GLOSSARY:

felt like scarecrows:	because they lacked new uniforms and equipment
Pommard:	a red wine from Burgundy in France
cashiering:	dismissal from the army
The Red Lamp:	the sign of an army brothel for privates and N.C.O.s; officers' brothels were indicated by blue lamps (see page 151)
assistant provost-marshal:	an officer employed on police duties behind the lines
a dose:	a venereal infection

'S'il vous plaît . . .': *(French)* 'Please, take off your shift, dear.'

'Oh, no'-non . . .': *(French)* 'Oh, no, no, lieutenant, that isn't decent.'

Laventie: a town near Armentières, further north than Béthune

the Prince of Wales: the eldest son (1894–1972) of George V, whom he succeeded, as Edward VIII, in 1936; he abdicated in the same year

Fortieth Siege Battery: a heavy artillery unit, used for long-range bombardment

A.S.C.: Army Service Corps

Third Battalion: the depot battalion, permanently stationed in Britain, used as a source of replacements for the fighting battalions abroad

R.S.M.: Regimental Sergeant Major

Nineteenth Brigade: brigades usually consisted of three or four battalions, often from different regiments; two or three brigades were formed into divisions, which were in turn grouped into corps

the Retreat: the 1914 retreat from Mons by the British forces

Fromelles: another town involved in the Aubers Ridge attack of May 1915

khaki-blancoed: blanco was a paste applied to straps and belts to whiten them for parades; khaki-blanco was applied to combat equipment

a battalion mess: all the officers dined together, instead of each company's dining in separate groups

château: *(French)* castle or mansion

the Field: a magazine of hunting and outdoor sports

Buzz Off: a rude way of telling someone to go away

Yarmouth: a fishing port on·the east coast of England

wart: a contemptuous nickname for an inferior officer, borrowed from public school slang

a wind-up tunic: in 1914, British officers wore their rank badges on conspicuous cuff-patches, but later these were transferred to the shoulder straps and made less obvious, partly because of disproportionate officer casualties (see page 194); the second-in-command is implying that officers who wear this kind of tunic are afraid to show their rank

parados: the back lip of the trench, opposite the parapet

intelligence officer: the officer who collected information about the enemy

sap-head: the end of a sap or trench dug out into No Man's Land

bowie-knife: a long-bladed knife, named after the American frontiersman and soldier, James Bowie (1796–1836)

Sir Pyers Mostyn: Welsh baronet (1895–1917)

'keeping a dog and barking themselves': doing something someone else should

a percussion bomb: one which explodes on hitting the target (see page 159)

Lowland territorials: auxiliary troops from the Lowlands of Scotland

atrocities to avenge: the Canadians claimed they had found one of their men crucified with bayonets by the Germans (see page 154); the grievance of the Scots is less well known

wicked: wickedly, with criminal negligence

traversing: sweeping its fire along the parapet of the trench

open five rounds rapid: fire five shots in quick succession; from an average platoon this would mean a hail of two hundred bullets in about twenty seconds

oak-leaf badge: the sign of a marksman

elephant-gun: a rifle normally used to shoot elephants and correspondingly large and powerful

Fortnum and Mason: the large London store, specialists in mail orders of parcels of rich food

West End: the fashionable part of London, where there are many theatres and restaurants

dug-out: over-age, but recalled to service because of the war

Lord Kitchener: Horatio Herbert Kitchener (1850–1916), made an earl in 1914; soldier and Minister of War, 1914–16

brigadier: officer commanding a brigade

became: mistake for 'obtained'

Neueste Nachrichten: (*German*) 'Latest News'

Lille: a French fortress town on the Belgian border, held by the Germans from 1914 to 1918

Warsaw: the capital city of Poland, taken by the Germans from the Russians, 5 August 1915

Christmas 1914:   on Christmas Day, 1914, Allied and German troops in the trenches ceased fire and met in No Man's Land to celebrate; Graves gives a fuller description in his short story 'Christmas Time' in *The Shout and Other Stories*, Penguin Books, Harmondsworth, 1965, pages 99–115

cold feet: (*colloquial*) cowardly reluctance

'Merry Widow' waltz: the waltz from the light opera *Die Lustige Witwe* ('The Merry Widow'), 1905, by Franz Lehár (1870–1948), Hungarian composer

night-lines: prearranged firing directions

'Wie geht's Ihnen, Kameraden?': (*German*) 'How are you, comrades?'

'Ach, Tommee, hast du denn deutsch gelernt?': (*German*) 'Ah, Tommy, have you learnt German, then?'

'Les sheunes madamoiselles...': (*French*, with German pronunciation) 'The young ladies of La Bassée [are] good to sleep with. The ladies of Béthune good too, eh?'

the Kaiser: the German Emperor Wilhelm II (1859–1941); he abdicated in 1918

the Crown Prince: Wilhelm (1882–1951), the heir to the German throne; he commanded a German army on the Western Front during the war

b———r: bugger (an expression of impatient disgust)

Die Wacht am Rhein: 'The Watch on the Rhine [a German river]', a popular German patriotic song

Louis XVI: the reign of Louis XVI, king of France, 1774–91, was a period of elegant furniture and interior decoration

Château Montmorency: not identified, though Graves implies it was near Béthune

---

Chapter 15

Graves on leave; then takes part in the Battle of Loos, September 1915 – a disaster.

NOTES AND GLOSSARY:

the appearance of cavalry: mounted troops were only positioned near the trenches before a big infantry attack, in the hope that a gap in the enemy line would be created for the cavalry to charge through

Cross: Richard Banastre Crosse (*b.*1888), D.S.O. and bar

Enlistment remained voluntary: see notes to Chapters 10 and 25

German Consul-General: official German representative in Britain

Scotland Yard: the police headquarters in London

Zeppelin scare: in January 1915 the Germans began long-range bombing missions against English cities by airships designed and built by Count Ferdinand von Zeppelin (1838–1917)

'The Actor': Graves's nickname for a fellow-officer

shows: here with its civilian meaning, a stage entertainment

driving bands: each shell had a copper ring round it to give a tighter fit in the gun barrel

skite: (*slang*) nonsense

Pimp: literally, a whoremaster or prostitutes' procurer

red tabs: red cloth patches worn by staff officers on their lapels; Graves quotes a traditional rhyme describing the archetypal staff officer

Hohenzollern Redoubt: a major German fortified position north of Loos, taken by the British, 25 September 1915, but lost again on 3 October; the Hohenzollerns were the royal family of Prussia and later of Germany

pioneers: soldiers specialising in engineering tasks like trench-building, usually too valuable to risk in an attack

iodine: used as an antiseptic for wounds

Platoon screens: large markers, easily visible from the air, to show the platoon's position

Mons Angels: Graves's footnote explains this incident of August 1914

The Last Supper: the last meal of Jesus and his disciples before the Crucifixion, a favourite subject of European painters

Marlborough: John Churchill, Duke of Marlborough (1650–1722), the greatest British general; in 1711 he penetrated a line of French defences before Cambrai not by a costly frontal assault but by brilliant and bloodless manoeuvring

G.S.O.1: General Staff Officer 1, a senior staff or planning officer

sods: (*slang*) men

iron rations: the emergency food supplies each man carried into battle

balls-up: (*slang*) confused failure

the Midlands: the central part of England, including several large industrial cities. Although regiments had geographical titles, their recruits could come from anywhere in Britain

***When we've Wound up the Watch on the Rhine*:** a song mocking the German patriotic one mentioned at the end of the previous chapter

***coal-box*:** another kind of large German projectile (compare 'sausage mortar-bomb', page 96)

***Kayser*:** an anglicised version of 'Kaiser' (pronounced 'Kyzer' in German)

***Allmands*:** Germans (from the French 'Allemands')

casualty clearing-station: a medical post where casualties were brought for examination. They were divided into three categories: those who could be sent to hospital (sometimes in Britain), those who could be

	successfully operated upon immediately, and those who could neither travel nor be treated on the spot; they were left to die, like Graves in Chapter 20
'Right of the Line':	traditionally, the most coveted position in the line of battle was on the extreme right, but this was, like the linear formation itself, quite obsolete by 1915
five-point-nines:	150 mm calibre howitzers, the most common German artillery
Dead calm:	at this stage of the war, both sides relied on the wind to blow poison gas to the enemy
set alight as a barrier:	in the hope that the heat would cause an air up-draught, taking the gas with it
Jäger:	(*German*) literally, 'hunters', because traditionally German light infantry had been recruited from foresters, gamekeepers and other rifle-users
Kingston:	the capital of the island of Jamaica, in the West Indies, then a British colony
'Jack Johnsons':	named after Jack Johnson (1878–1946), an American boxer, the first black world Heavyweight Champion, 1908–15
Jocks:	Scottish soldiers, both Lowlanders (in trousers) and Highlanders in kilts (hence 'bare-arsed')
skite:	(*slang*) run away
whistled:	officers used whistles to convey orders to their men
wallah:	operator or man in charge (from a Hindu word)
gas-pipes:	(*slang*) mortars
Vermorel-sprayers:	Vermoral-sprayers were used to spray a chemical composition over lingering gas to neutralise it
a runner:	a soldier carrying a message
lyddite:	an explosive, named after Lydd, in Kent, where it was first tested in the late nineteenth century
Hill 70:	a map reference to a terrain feature behind Loos
Highland Division:	the 51st Division, made up of Scottish Highlanders
Ian Hay:	Major-General John Hay Beith (1876–1952), Scottish soldier and author; his book, *The First Hundred Thousand* (1915), one of the first about the war, describes the battle of Loos, but at no point does he say his men were 'let down' by anybody
flat caps:	soldiers wearing the peaked soft service cap; some British troops, like the Highlanders, wore other forms of hat (steel helmets were not yet in use). Hay refers in his book to 'flat heads' (page 331), but never uses the phrase Graves quotes
done for:	(*slang*) killed

morphia:	an opiate, used as a pain-killer
a cup final:	a well-attended football match
roley-poley:	a kind of pudding
Sailly la Bourse:	a village two miles west of Cambrin
Annezin:	a small village west of Béthune

Chapter 16

Trench-warfare, 1916; Graves meets Siegfried Sassoon.

NOTES AND GLOSSARY:

Maire:	(*French*) 'Mayor'
Fouquières:	a village a few miles south-west of Béthune
the other war:	the Franco-Prussian War, 1870–1
petit-caporal:	(*French*) 'little corporal'; perhaps Graves means a lance-corporal
Pas de Calais:	the area around Calais, a port in north-east France
estaminets:	(*French*) small restaurants
Versailles Treaty:	the peace treaty between the Allies and Germany, 28 June 1919; the Germans agreed to pay compensation for war damage
over the top:	over the trench parapet and into No Man's Land, the first steps in an attack
'mad-minute':	a short, intense burst of firing
going west:	(*slang*) being killed
Charles Sorley:	Scottish-born poet (1895–1915)
Isaac Rosenberg:	English poet (1890–1918), notable for serving in the ranks, rather than as an officer, in the King's Own Royal Lancasters
Wilfred Owen:	English poet (1893–1918), officer in the Manchester Regiment; see the end of Chapter 24
gazetted:	listed in the *London Gazette*, the official record of promotions; in fact Graves was promoted to captain on 26 October 1915
stars:	a British Army captain's rank is indicated by three stars
sappers:	military engineers
a daily exchange of courtesies:	other reports of rhythmical machine-gun fire are noted in Tony Ashworth: *Trench Warfare 1914–1918*, London, 1980, pages 116–17, although, as Paul Fussell says, the guns could not fire if cartridges were missing, so that Graves's explanation is mistaken
Piccadilly:	a place in central London
drawers:	knickers or underpants

John Bull: a magazine, started in 1906 by Horatio Bottomley (1860–1933), specialising in scandal and crude patriotism

'a certain proposal': a euphemism for homosexual soliciting

neurasthenia: (*Greek*) literally, 'nerve-weakness', the term for combat fatigue during and after the First World War

Dr W. H. R. Rivers: English psychologist and anthropologist (1864–1922); see Chapter 24

'whether the cow calved . . .': whether things went well or badly

puttees: cloth strips wound round the leg between knee and ankle; from a Hindu word for bandages

Bouchavesnes: a town in northern France five miles north of Péronne, taken by the French, September 1916

dismounted cavalry: cavalry served as infantry in the trenches because of the demand for reinforcements and the unlikelihood of a cavalry breakthrough

French-yellow: a dull greenish-yellow

Locon: a town four miles north of Béthune

Livers were better: because less alcohol was drunk by the officers

The Essays of Lionel Johnson: *Postliminium* (1912), a book of essays by Lionel Johnson (1867–1902), minor poet and critic

Keats: John Keats (1795–1821), English romantic poet

Blake: William Blake (1757–1827), English poet and painter

Siegfried Sassoon: English poet (1886–1967); in his semi-fictionalised *Memoirs of an Infantry Officer* (1930) he gives his version of his friendship with Graves, whom he there calls 'David Cromlech'

eighteen-ninetyish flavour: the decadent, late romantic style of the end of the nineteenth century

Over the Brazier: published in 1916

Return to greet me . . .: the opening stanza of Sassoon's poem 'To Victory' (4 January 1916), dedicated to Edmund Gosse (1849–1928), the English literary critic

Tottie Fay: there was no actress of this name, but there was a slang expression 'Tottie fie'; a tottie was a smart young woman, sometimes a prostitute

Birmingham: an industrial city in the English Midlands

Field Punishment No 1: the victim's outspread arms were tied to some fixed object, such as a wagon wheel; more humiliating than painful

'buckshee': (*Army slang*) usually means 'free or extra'; its meaning here is obscure

Military Service Act: this finally introduced conscription in Britain, January, 1916

and Bar: denoting a second award of the same medal

Médaille Militaire: (*French*) 'military medal'

reduced for drunkenness: punished for drunkenness by being made a private again

stripes: sergeant's rank badges (three cloth chevrons on the sleeve)

***Memoirs of a Fox-hunting Man*:** the first part of Sassoon's fictionalised autobiography, published in 1928; Graves refers to Part 10, section II, pages 251–3

***Hommes 40, chevaux 8*:** (*French*) '40 men, 8 horses'; the capacity of the railway trucks when carrying either load

Picardy: the region of France south of Amiens

***Comment Vivre Cent Ans*:** (*French*) 'How to live for a hundred years'

Longfellow's *Evangeline*: a poem published in 1847 by the American poet Henry Wadsworth Longfellow (1807–82)

Colonel Ford: J. R. Minshull-Ford (1881–1948), later Major-General, commanded First Royal Welch Fusiliers, 1914–15 and 1916

field day: a day spent on battle training in the open countryside

full-back ... front row scrum-man ... fly-half ... inside three-quarter: various team positions in rugby

the axe: (*slang*) the trouble

***Jack*:** actually an Army slang term for a corporal

***delirium tremens*:** (*Latin*) 'trembling madness', reputedly the last stage of alcoholism

Jacquot: (*French*) Jack

Amiens: a town in France north of Paris

Abbeville: a town north-west of Amiens

Rouen: a town between Paris and the north coast of France

Chapter 17

Graves becomes an instructor at Harfleur; general comments on soldiers and the war.

NOTES AND GLOSSARY:

'Bull Ring': the nickname for a large training camp

trench relief: the replacement of one battalion by another in the front line, a period of great danger if the enemy attacked

storm-troops: soldiers specially trained to lead attacks, part of the German answer to the stalemate of trench warfare

Yorkshire, Lancashire: the largest industrial counties of the north of England

Ulstermen: men from Northern Ireland

Catholic Irish: mainly from the southern part of Ireland

Highland Scots: from the mountainous northern part of Scotland, and, like the Catholic Irish, a Celtic people

overseas troops: soldiers from the British Empire, including Canadians, Australians, New Zealanders and Indians

Algerians: Algeria was then a French colony

Portuguese: Portugal entered the war on the Allied side in March 1916; although she hoped to gain some of Germany's African colonies, she had no real reason for becoming involved

an early Russian cavalry raid: at the very start of the war, before the Russian defeats at Tannenberg and the Masurian Lakes in Poland, August 1914, the Russians made some cavalry raids in East Prussia

franc-tireurs: the French term for a guerilla or terrorist

apt to turn on striking: not penetrating cleanly, but being deflected so that the bullet entered the flesh sideways, lacerating it

Canadian-Scot: many Scots emigrated to Canada in the nineteenth century; they formed Scottish-style regiments (even wearing kilts) when the war came

a Mills bomb: a hand grenade

the pin: a metal prong which once extracted sets the grenade to explode

Morlancourt: a town in northern France a few miles south of Albert

Camarades: anglicised version of 'Kameraden' ('comrades'), the German cry of surrender

all dinkum: (*Australian*) all very nice

Turcos: French Algerian troops, noted for their cruelty

the Marne: the river near Paris which was the limit of the German advance in 1914

'*Et enfin, ces animaux*...': (*French*) 'And finally those beasts tore off their ears and put them in their pockets!'

Flixécourt: a town on the Somme river between Amiens and Abbeville

pozzy: (*Army slang*) jam

napoo: (*Army slang*) finished, ended, gone

next door: neighbouring

sloping and ordering arms: drill movements with the rifle: placing it over the shoulder, and holding it by your side

the Guards:	still famous for their parade drill
'bible-wallahs':	a slang term for strict Christians
Gott:	German for 'God'
Anglican:	belonging to the Church of England
the cloth:	the clergy, so called from the traditional black clothing they wear (though army chaplains wear uniform)
extreme unction:	a ritual anointing performed by Roman Catholic priests on those of their faith about to die
push:	(*slang*) military offensive
Mesopotamia:	modern Iraq, where the British were fighting the Turks for control of the oil-fields
commutation of tithes:	the substitution of money for produce in gifts to support the clergy

Chapter 18

Trench warfare on the Somme, March-April, 1916.

NOTES AND GLOSSARY:

'*Triste, la guerre!*':	(*French*) 'Sad, the war!'
ammonal:	an explosive mixture of ammonium nitrate, powdered aluminium and trinitrotoluene
the Day of Judgement:	the end of the world, when Christians believe God will come to judge mankind
Trafalgar Square:	another famous London place-name applied to a part of the trench system
Touch wood:	a superstitious ritual to avert a bad omen
unrevetted:	not shored up with timber
Glamorgan:	a county in south Wales
tracheotomy:	a throat operation to make an opening in the windpipe
Eight:	an eight-man rowing boat
Radley:	an English public school
***le jeune capitaine*:**	(*French*) 'the young captain'
'He that shall endure...':	from the Bible, Mark 13:13
'To an inheritance...':	from the Bible, I Peter 1:4–5
trump:	(*archaic*) trumpet
septum:	partition of bone and cartilage in the nose, dividing it into two narrow cavities
the expected offensive:	the British attack on the Somme river, which began on 1 July 1916
C. D. Morgan:	no further information discovered

Chapter 19

Graves, on leave, attends church for the last time; he returns to the front during a raid.

NOTES AND GLOSSARY:

Good Friday: the Friday before Easter Sunday, regarded by Christians as the anniversary of Christ's crucifixion

matins: morning service in the Church of England

Herodotus: Greek historian (*c.*480–*c.*425BC); Graves refers to the first book of his *History*, section 31

Solon: Greek legislator (*c.*638–*c.*558BC)

King Croesus: last king of Lydia (sixth century BC); when he boasted of his happiness, Solon replied that no man could be called happy until he died happy

Holy Communion: the ritual consumption of bread and wine in commemoration of Christ's last meal and his self-sacrifice afterwards

clericus: (*Latin*) 'clergyman'; the 'i' is short. Graves goes on to imitate his speaking voice mockingly

took the Sacrament: participated in Holy Communion

guineas: professional men, such as doctors and lawyers, continued to state their fees in guineas (each worth twenty-one shillings), although the coin was no longer in use

psalm: a religious poem or hymn, especially one from the Book of Psalms in the Old Testament of the Bible; Graves quotes from the 121st

Honourable Cymmrodorion Society: founded in 1873

W. M. Hughes: Australian politician (1862–1952), Prime Minister of Australia, 1915–23

Mersey: the river which flows past Liverpool and makes it a major port

Light or vintage: kinds of port wine

Bacon: Sir Francis Bacon (1561–1626), politician and scientific writer, thought by some to be the real author of the plays attributed to the less educated Shakespeare

Hilaire Belloc: French-born English writer and poet (1870–1953), who wrote and lectured on the course of the war as it happened

Gilbert and Sullivan: W. S. Gilbert (1836–1911) and Sir Arthur Sullivan (1842–1900) wrote the words and music for a series of operettas between 1875 and 1896

the regimental harper: the harp is regarded as a traditional Welsh
instrument

the Twelfth: the twelfth of August, the day on which the grouse-shooting season opens

with a stone: rather than with a sporting gun

hunt: a body of foxhunters with a pack of foxhounds

St Andrews: the University of St Andrews, the oldest in Scotland

the Lincolnshire: a horse race, traditionally run at Lincoln, in eastern England

Bootle: a small town near Liverpool

affiliation orders: legal determination of the paternity of illegitimate children

the Somme offensive: the biggest offensive yet attempted by the British Army; it continued until November 1916 but made small gains for huge casualties (see Chapter 20)

Red Dragon: a Welsh emblem, found on the flag of Wales

the *Lusitania*: an ocean liner, sunk by a German submarine off Ireland, 5 May 1915; 128 Americans were killed

the Yanks: (*slang*) the Americans; the United States did not declare war on Germany until 6 April 1917

'jumped-up': (*slang*) undeservedly promoted

one star: a single star was the rank badge of a second lieutenant

Carl Graves: Armgaard Karl Graves was tried and sentenced for spying in Scotland, July 1912; he was released before the war began

Zürich: in Switzerland, a neutral country throughout the war

trooper: cavalry soldier

D.S.O.: Distinguished Service Order, an award for bravery given to officers; the Distinguished Conduct Medal was for other ranks

Chapter 20

The Somme, July 1916: the attack on High Wood. Graves is seriously wounded.

NOTES AND GLOSSARY:

Daours: a town on the river Aincre a few miles east of Amiens

Buire: another town on the Aincre, a few miles south-west of Albert

'Happy Valley': an ironic nickname

Mametz Wood: on the Somme front near Albert; captured 12 July 1916

Siegfried distinguished himself: see Sassoon's *Memoirs of an Infantry Officer*, Part 4

a rhymed letter: 'Letter to S.S. from Mametz Wood' in *Fairies and Fusiliers* (1917), Graves's answer to Sassoon's 'A Letter Home', May 1916, published in *The Old Huntsman* (1917)

Stockpot: a nickname for Stockwell, the colonel commanding the First Battalion, Royal Welch Fusiliers

C.B.: Commander of the Bath, the lowest of the three classes of the Order of the Bath

Lehr Regiment: a German regiment specialising in training demonstrations

I was still superstitious about looting...: three pages later, however, Graves describes a souvenir he sent to Dr Dunn

Martinpuich: a town between Albert and Bapaume, taken by the British on 15 September 1916

Bazentin-le-Petit: a village south of Martinpuich, taken 14 July 1916

Tyneside Irish: the 103rd Brigade, consisting of four battalions of Royal Northumberland Fusiliers (24th, 25th, 26th and 27th), all made up of Irish workers from northeast England

one for sorrow: part of a superstitious rhyme assigning meanings to the numbers of magpies seen at one time

a hot-cross bun: an Easter-time spiced bread roll, decorated on top with a pastry cross; from above, it appears as a circle enclosing a cross

Public Schools Battalion: officially the 20th Battalion, Royal Fusiliers

the Central Powers: Germany and Austria-Hungary (and later their allies Turkey and Bulgaria), so called because of their geographical position in the centre of Europe, between France and Russia

practising: working as a doctor

Glasgow: a city in Scotland

O.C.: officer commanding

Co.: company

S14b: a map reference

X roads: short for 'cross roads'

legged it: (*slang*) ran away

French 75's: French 75 mm calibre field guns

artillery formation: the formation infantry used when advancing under artillery fire; small groups of men spaced out in a diamond-shaped pattern

'*Anglais no bon...*': (*mixed French and English*) 'English no good, Germans very good. War finish, English defeated. Germans win.'

six- and eight-inch: the diameters of the shells fired

Nietzsche: Friedrich Wilhelm Nietzsche (1844–1900), German philosopher and poet

Non, tu ne me peux pas tuer!: (*French*) 'No, you cannot kill me!', a translation of the line 'Sterben? Sterben kann ich nicht!' ('Die? I cannot die!') from Nietzsche's poem 'Yorick als Zigeuner' (1884)

William le Queux: English writer (1864–1927), specialising in stories predicting future wars, particularly between Britain and Germany

Heilly: a town on the Aincre ten miles east of Amiens

Lt-Col.: Lieutenant-Colonel

brigade-major: a staff officer attached to a brigade; his account of the battle, implying that only the Royal Welch Fusiliers held their positions, angered Scottish soldiers in particular, so that Graves added the next paragraph to the second edition

R.C.: Roman Catholic

Captain Colbart: Lieutenant J. S. Coltart (*sic*) was the senior surviving officer of the 5th Scottish Rifles when the Royal Welch Fusiliers entered High Wood; he became a captain later

R.A.M.C.: Royal Army Medical Corps; on the next page Graves gives a satirical expansion of these initials, referring to the theft of the wounded men's personal possessions when in hospital

your number was up: (*slang*) you were bound to die

the Last Post: the bugle call which ends the army day

Webley: a type of pistol, rather large and heavy

Gazette de Rouen: (*French*) *The Rouen Gazette*, the local newspaper

---

Chapter 21

Graves recovers. Attitudes to the war.

NOTES AND GLOSSARY:

Queen Alexandra's Hospital: a hospital named after Edward VII's queen (1844–1925)

Highgate: part of north London

Sir Alfred Mond: Industrialist, financier and Member of Parliament (1868–1930)

my supposed death: Graves was listed as 'Died of Wounds' on page 5 of *The Times*, 4 August 1916

Court Circular: the part of a newspaper which reports on royal engagements, official functions and society weddings

Criccieth: a town in Wales, where the Lloyd Georges had a house

Post-corporal: corporal in charge of mail

Cox's Bank: Cox and Co., opened in 1758 by Richard Cox (1718–1803) as Army Pay Agents; taken over by Lloyds Bank in 1923

Paddington Station: a London main-line station

***The Morning Post*:** a British national newspaper

Her Majesty: Queen Mary (1867–1953), King George V's wife

Tommy Atkins: the rather obvious pseudonym adopted by the 'Common Soldier' (see notes to Chapter 11)

inst.: (*Latin*) 'instant', meaning 'this month'

'comfy': short for 'comfortable'

the apple of our eye: our dearly loved child

report: school report

***To face the music*:** to confront danger

Rachel the Silent: Rachel, wife of Jacob in the Bible, Genesis 29–35; elsewhere there are references to her 'weeping for her children' (Jeremiah 31:15; Matthew 2:18), although she is not called 'the Silent'

***The Gentlewoman*:** a ladies' magazine

***The Star*:** a newspaper

wards: rooms in a hospital

***Hospital Blue*:** a wounded soldier, so called from the blue clothing worn by patients in military hospitals

Florence Nightingale: nurse and hospital administrator (1820–1910), famous for her efforts to help the wounded in the Crimean War

***Percival H. Monkton*:** no further information discovered

First Battalion friend: in fact this was Sassoon, who was greatly offended by this passage in *Goodbye to All That*

the Dardanelles: the southern part of the sea passage between the Mediterranean and Black Seas; the British tried to seize it from the Turks in 1915

spiritualistic means: spiritualism, the belief that the spirits of the dead can communicate with the living, understandably became common among relatives of dead soldiers in the First World War

Formby: a small town on the coast north of Liverpool

Royal St David's: a golf club in Harlech
iron: a metal club for striking the golf ball
links: a golf course among dunes near a seashore
Adelphi Hotel: large hotel in Liverpool
Beaumont-Hamel: a town a few miles north of Albert, taken by the British, 13 November 1916
as long as a cricket pitch: twenty-two yards
India paper: very thin paper
Catullus: see Chapter 5, page 35
Lucretius: Titus Lucretius Carus (*c*.99–*c*.55BC), Roman philosophical poet
***Drapeau Blanc*:** (*French*) 'white flag', the name of a brothel
dummies: straw-filled sacks for bayonet practice
privates: genitals

Chapter 22

Graves returns to France, 1917, but is sent home as unfit.

NOTES AND GLOSSARY:
Frises: probably Frise, a village on the river Somme five miles west of Péronne; the southern end of the British-held line in 1917
General Pinney: Major-General Sir Reginald Pinney (1863–1943) commanded the 33rd Division from 1916 to 1919
teetotal: against alcoholic drinks
Cléry: a town on the Somme near Péronne, taken by the French, 3 September 1916
Suzanne: another town on the Somme, near Bray
the House of Commons: the lower house of the British Parliament
'The bed is too narrow . . .': 'For the bed is shorter than that a man can stretch himself on it: and the covering narrower than that he can wrap himself in it' (Isaiah 28:20)
***Are ye there . . .*:** misquoted lines from the second stanza of Kipling's poem 'Chant-Pagan (English Irregular Discharged)' from *Service Songs* (1903)
AA202: the reference number of a previous order
B.Echelon: the supply services
Scots Greys: a cavalry regiment, famous for riding grey horses

---

Chapter 23

Graves goes to Oxford, where he meets many writers, and to the Isle of Wight.

NOTES AND GLOSSARY:

Somerville College: the University of Oxford is in fact an association of different colleges, each with its own buildings and traditions; Somerville College, one of the most recent, was founded in 1879

Examination Schools: the halls where examinations were held

boarded: passed fit by a medical board (see page 194)

status quo ante: (*Latin*) 'the state of things before'; that is, a return to pre-war conditions, without change

the Liberal Government: the Liberal Party continued in office after the outbreak of war, but in May 1915 was replaced by a government also containing members of other political parties and eventually led by Lloyd George

between trade-rivals: a major reason for British hostility to Germany was the latter's challenge to Britain's industrial and commercial supremacy

the Jesses, not the Davids: in the Bible (I Samuel 17), David, the youngest son of Jesse, slays the Philistine giant Goliath in single combat

Tipperary: a popular marching song of the First World War

Salmon: David's great-great-grandfather, not his uncle; see the Bible, Ruth 4:20–22

Wadham: Wadham College, Oxford, founded in 1612

General Solly-Flood: Major-General Arthur Solly-Flood (1871–1940)

Fiji: a Pacific island, then a British colony

the senior common-room: a club for university staff members

Stenning: John Frederick Stenning (1868–1959), Fellow of Wadham College, Reader in Aramaic (not Hebrew)

a fellow: a member of a college at Oxford or a similarly organised university

J. V. Powell: John Undershell Powell (1865–1936), Fellow of St John's from 1891 to his death

college scout: a servant

Rhodes Scholars: Cecil Rhodes (1853–1902), South African politician and diamond-mine owner, left money in his will to provide scholarships for foreign students at Oxford

Aldous Huxley: English novelist (1894–1963)

Wilfred Childe: English poet and academic (1890–1952)

Thomas Earp: English writer (1892–1958)

St Giles's: a main street in Oxford

Cornmarket: another street in Oxford

the Cadena: a cafe in the Cornmarket, Oxford, one of a chain of the same name throughout England; it closed during the 1960s

Garsington: a village a few miles south-east of Oxford

The Morrells: Philip Morrell (1870–1943) and his wife Ottoline (1872–1938) were the centre of a wide circle of writers and artists, who frequently stayed at their house, Garsington Manor

Clive Bell: English critic and art theorist (1881–1964)

a conscientious objector: someone who refuses on ethical grounds to be conscripted into the army

Lytton Strachey: English historical biographer (1880–1932)

Bertrand Russell: later third Earl Russell (1872–1970), English mathematician and philosopher

Osbert . . . Sitwell: English poet and writer (1892–1969); he served throughout the war in the Grenadier Guards

Sacheverell Sitwell: Osbert's younger brother (*b.*1897), poet, critic and traveller; he joined the Grenadier Guards in 1917

Herbert Read: English poet and critic (1893–1968); his writings include accounts of his war service with the Green Howards

George Moore: Irish novelist (1852–1933); his novel *The Brook Kerith* (1916) re-tells the story of Jesus Christ, thus anticipating Graves's own novel *King Jesus* (1946)

the Reform Club: a London gentleman's club

'Mr Britling': in 1916 H. G. Wells (1866–1946) published a novel about the war called *Mr Britling Sees it Through*

'Cook's Tour': Thomas Cook (1808–92) invented the organised excursion or package tour holiday; Graves applies the term in contempt to Government-arranged visits to the trenches by civilians

Arnold Bennett: English novelist (1867–1931)

Augustine Birrell: English literary critic (1850–1933), chief secretary for Ireland (not Lord Lieutenant) 1907–16

the Apocrypha: certain religious books associated with the Bible but excluded from it as not divinely inspired

Elihu the Jebusite: in the Book of Job, chapters 32–37

Job's comforters: an ironic title for Eliphaz of Teman, Bildad of Shuah and Zophar of Naamath, the unsympathetic friends of Job who tell him his misfortunes are a divine punishment

John Galsworthy: English novelist and playwright (1867–1933)

Reveille: a literary magazine, edited by Galsworthy, 1918–19

Ivor Novello: English songwriter and actor (1893–1951)

Royal Navy Air Service: the Royal Naval Air Service, the Royal Navy's flying unit

Isle of Wight: a large island off the south coast of England

Osborne Palace: Osborne House, Queen Victoria's favourite home, where she died in 1901; it is still used as a convalescent hospital

the Prince Consort: Queen Victoria's husband, Prince Albert of Saxe-Cóburg-Gotha (1819–61); he helped to design Osborne House

Winterhalters: royal portraits by the German painter Franz Xavier Winterhalter (1806–73)

Cowes: a harbour town in the north of the Isle of Wight, a centre for yachting

Royal Yacht Squadron: the leading British yacht club

the Solent: the sea channel between the Isle of Wight and the mainland, a favourite place for yacht racing

Benedictine Fathers: monks of the order established by St Bernard (AD480–543)

Solesmes: a town near Cambrai in north-east France

Quarr: in the north-east of the Isle of Wight

the Vatican: the Pope's palace in Rome, the administrative centre of Roman Catholic Christianity

Freemason: the Freemasons are an all-male secret society, often accused of conspiracy and immorality, especially by the Roman Catholic Church

Joffre: Joseph Joffre (1852–1931), French commander-in-chief from 1914 to 1916

Foch: Ferdinand Foch (1851–1929), French general, made Supreme Allied Commander in France from March 1918 until the end of the war

Guest-master: the monk appointed to entertain visitors

black-letter: an early form of printing, usually pre-1600

bon catholique: (*French*) 'good catholic'

Peut-être après la guerre: (*French*) 'perhaps after the war'

Promenade, mademoiselle?: (*French*) 'a walk, young lady?'

The Lives of the Saints: there are many books of lives of the saints; one of the best-known is that written by James of Voragine (*d. c.*1298), called *The Golden Legend* in English

A. A. Milne: English writer (1882–1956), mainly of comic and children's books

Vernon Bartlett: Charles Vernon Oldfield Bartlett (*b.*1894), English author and M.P.

a Scottish dirk: a small knife, often worn as part of Highland dress; Prince Albert had been a frequent visitor to Scotland with Queen Victoria

Hessian: from Hesse, one of the states of Germany; Prince Albert was a German

side-whiskers:	a mid-nineteenth-century hair-style followed by Prince Albert
Alberta:	a large province in central Canada, established in 1882 and made a province in 1905
Albert Nyanza:	Lake Albert, in Africa, lately known as Lake Mobutu
Albert Medal:	a medal for bravery awarded to civilians rather than servicemen; equivalent to the Victoria Cross
Albert Memorial:	the monument to Prince Albert in Kensington Gardens, London
Albert Docks:	the Royal Albert Dock, London
Aldershot:	a town south-west of London, site of a large army barracks
John Brown:	Queen Victoria's personal servant or 'ghillie' (1826–83) at her Scottish castle of Balmoral, near Aberdeen
'alf:	half
the coroner:	the English magistrate responsible for investigating the causes of deaths

Chapter 24

Sassoon and his protest against the war, July 1917.

NOTES AND GLOSSARY:

the black mare:	see Sassoon's *Memoirs of a Fox-hunting Man*, Part 10, section III
***The Nation*:**	a magazine, founded as *The Speaker* in 1890, which became *The Nation* in 1907, merged with *The Athenaeum* in 1921 and with the *New Statesman* in 1931; its chief editor was H. W. Massingham (1860–1924)
...*Rapture and pale Enchantment*:	from Sassoon's poem 'Conscripts'
House of Lords:	the upper chamber of the British Parliament, consisting at this time of hereditary noblemen and some senior clergy
Heavy fighting in the Hindenburg Line:	for Sassoon's version of the incident mentioned by Graves, see *Memoirs of an Infantry Officer*, Part 8, section IV
Fontaine-les-Croiselles:	a town south-east of Arras, involved in the Battle of Arras, April 1917
the Premier:	the Prime Minister, Lloyd George
Sir Douglas Haig:	General (later Field Marshal) Sir Douglas Haig (1861–1928), commander-in-chief of the British army in France, 1916–19

Richard Dadd: English painter (1819–87) who went insane
Hyde Park: a park in central London containing a lake called the Serpentine
Vimy: a low ridge north of Arras captured from the Germans by Canadian troops, 9 April 1917
'Oh, life, oh, sun!': the last words of Graves's poem 'Escape'
Barbusse: Henri Barbusse (1873–1935), French author of a novel about his war service, *Le Feu* (1916), translated as *Under Fire*
playing to the gallery: doing something for the sake of gaining applause
***Bradford Pioneer*:** a newspaper; Bradford is a town in the north of England
C.O.s: conscientious objectors
***Philip Frankford*:** not identified; perhaps a journalistic pseudonym
Clifford Allen: later Lord Allen of Hurtwood (1889–1939), a socialist and pacifist, three times imprisoned as a conscientious objector
Scott Duckers: probably James Scott Duckers (dates unknown), lawyer and poet
the political 'offenders' of Ireland: Irish nationalists; they had unsuccessfully rebelled against British rule in 1916
Evan Morgan: Evan Frederic Morgan, Viscount Tredegar (1893–1949), private secretary to the Parliamentary Secretary, Ministry of Labour, 1917
Lees-Smith: Hastings Bertrand Lees-Smith (1878–1941), Labour politician and Member of Parliament
the House: the House of Commons
Colonel Jones-Williams: Lt-Col. H. R. Jones-Williams (dates unknown)
Major Macartney-Filgate: Major A. R. P. Macartney-Filgate (dates unknown)
the Caucasus: a mountain range in Asia, between the Black and Caspian Seas
thrown his Military Cross into the sea: Sassoon's version is that he threw the medal ribbon only; he did not possess the actual medal (see *Memoirs of an Infantry Officer*, Parts 4 and 10)
ratting: (*slang*) betraying them
'S' stood for 'Siegfried': Sassoon's first name is German and might be taken as a sign of sympathy with the enemy
a 'duration of the war' captain: not a regular officer, but a volunteer serving only until the war ends
jesuitically: unscrupulously, as the Jesuits, a Roman Catholic religious order, are said to act to advance their cause in the world

Captain McDowell: possibly Robert John Stewart McDowall (*b*.1892), Scottish doctor and author, who served as a Major in the Royal Army Medical Corps

Harley Street: a street in London where many eminent and expensive doctors have consulting rooms

Edinburgh: the capital city of Scotland; Craiglockhart is one of its western suburbs

'Dottyville': (*slang*) 'crazytown'

London University parliamentary seat: certain British universities elected their own Members of Parliament at this time

Labour: the moderate socialist party founded in 1900 (though not called the Labour Party until 1906); by 1922 it had replaced the Liberals as the alternative to the Conservatives and in the next year formed its first government

Conflict and Dream: published in 1923

The Hydra: named after a creature in Greek mythology, a many-headed monster; as soon as one of its heads was cut off, two grew in its place

Counter-Attack: published in 1918; in Edinburgh Sassoon communicated his bitterness about the war, violently expressed in his poetry, to Wilfred Owen

---

Chapter 25

Graves serves in base camps in Britain; he marries Nancy Nicholson, January 1918.

NOTES AND GLOSSARY:

the Derby Scheme: a partial conscription, begun in October 1915, by which men were called up by categories to join the Army; but this did not provide enough recruits and was replaced in January 1916 by the Military Service Act, which introduced full conscription, except for certain essential workers

the 1918 spring: in March 1918 the Germans, using new tactics, began a series of successful attacks in France which threatened to win the war

T.N.T.: trinitrotoluene, used in making explosives

Lord Crewe: Robert Crewe-Milnes, Marquess of Crewe (1858–1945), English Liberal politician

Lord Carson: Sir Edward Carson, Baron Carson (1854–1935), Northern Irish lawyer and political leader

Oswestry: actually in England, though very near the Welsh border

58 · Summaries

Rhyl:	a town on the north coast of Wales
Nancy Nicholson:	Annie Mary Pryde Nicholson (1899–1977), a talented artist who later specialised in printed fabric designs
Ben:	Ben Nicholson (1894–1982), English painter
Chelsea:	a district of west-central London
Victoria Station:	a London station, from which trains go to the south coast and the ferries to France
Lee White:	American actress and singer (1886–1927); she appeared in *Cheep* in London in April 1917
'Girls must all be Farmers' Boys...':	because so many men were in the army, women took over their jobs, including farm labour (they were called Land Girls)
Stevenson's *Child's Garden of Verses*:	a book of poems for children, published in 1885 by the Scottish writer Robert Louis Stevenson (1850–94)
Mabel Nicholson:	Scottish painter (1871–1918); her maiden name was Pryde
William Nicholson:	Sir William Nicholson (1872–1949), English painter
Huntingdonshire:	a small county about sixty miles north of London
land-service:	farm labour
rot:	(*slang*) nonsense
Gibraltar:	the British-held port at the western entrance to the Mediterranean Sea
Cairo:	the capital city of Egypt; see Chapters 31 and 32
sortie:	a departure from port; the Germans had a powerful fleet, but an even larger British one kept it in port for most of the war
York:	a city in north-east England
Morse:	a telegraphic code invented by an American electrician, S. F. B. Morse (1791–1872)
dash-dot-dash-dash:	morse code for letter 'Y'
dash-dot-dash-dot:	morse code for letter 'C'
Cork:	a city in southern Ireland
the Easter Rebellion in 1916:	an unsuccessful rising, 24–9 April 1916, by Irish nationalists who hoped to end British rule in Ireland
Sinn Feiners:	members of Sinn Fein (*Irish*, pronounced 'Shin Fane') meaning 'ourselves alone', an Irish republican party, whose leaders were executed after the Easter Rising, 1916
crocks:	old and unfit men
Holyhead:	a town in north-west Wales, a port for ferries to southern Ireland

Russian Order of St Anne: founded in 1735; there were four classes and crossed swords indicated a military rather than a civil award

October Bolshevik revolution: the Bolsheviks, a revolutionary socialist party, seized power in Russia in late 1917, abolishing the Russian monarchy and making peace with Germany

a minor: not yet twenty-one years old and so too young to be legally independent of parental guidance

Sir James Fowler: English physician (1852–1934), specialist in lung diseases; served as a colonel in the army medical service at Rouen

so horrified that she all but refused: Nancy was probably outraged by the marriage service for sanctifying the husband's supremacy over the wife; contrast Graves's mother's attitude at the end of Chapter 4

aunts using handkerchiefs: conventionally, female relatives weep sentimentally at weddings

sugar and butter cards: documents showing entitlement to these rationed commodities

champagne: a white sparkling wine from France

E. V. Lucas: Edward Verrall Lucas (1868–1938), essayist and literary scholar

the present Archbishop of Wales: Alfred George Edwards (1848–1937), Archbishop of Wales, 1920–34

St Asaph: a town in north Wales

hippophagist: horse-eating

Langham's Hotel: probably the Langham Hotel, Portland Place, London, now closed

Bishop of Oxford: Thomas Banks Strong (1861–1944), Bishop of Oxford, 1925–37

Samuel Richardson: English novelist (1689–1761)

Bishop of Liverpool: Albert Augustus David (1867–1950), Bishop of Liverpool, 1923–44

Robbie Ross: Robert Ross (1869–1918), English writer and friend of Oscar Wilde

Oscar Wilde: Irish poet, playwright and critic (1854–1900); imprisoned for homosexual practices in 1895

Polygon Wood: five miles east of Ypres in Belgium; taken by the British in September and October 1917 during the battle known as Third Ypres or Passchendaele

The Companionage and Knightage: *Whitaker's Peerage, Baronetage, Knightage and Companionage*, an annual record of the aristocracy and other notable people

Issue: here means 'offspring' or 'children'; Old Joe takes it to mean what equipment the Army issued to him

Family seat: actually means 'ancestral home'

'When I'm asleep . . .': first line of Sassoon's poem 'Sick Leave' (October 1917)

To these I turn . . .: the first stanza of Sassoon's poem 'The Kiss' (April 1916)

Colonel Campbell, V.C.: both Graves and Sassoon name this officer, but the records of V.C. awards mention no-one of this name and rank in 1917

Yeomanry: militia cavalry

Ephraim: a mountain area north of Jerusalem

Morlancourt: the German offensive of spring, 1918, retook this town, where Sassoon had been billeted in earlier years; see page 154

Duhamel: Georges Duhamel (1884–1966), French novelist; the quotation is from his *Vie des Martyrs* (translated as *The New Book of Martyrs*, 1918), based on his work as an army surgeon

Tudor: the Tudor family ruled England from 1485 to 1603

Spanish influenza: this disease killed more people at the end of the First World War than the war itself

Siegfried had been shot through the head: see Sassoon's *Sherston's Progress*, Part 4, section 11

a verse-letter: Sassoon refused to let Graves use this in the first edition of *Goodbye to All That*, which appeared with several blank pages as a result; the poem is the 'Letter to Robert Graves' in Sassoon's *War Poems*, pages 130–3

Country Sentiment: published in 1920

Rhuddlan: a town in north Wales; not a battlefield, but the place where in 1284 Edward I, King of England (1272–1307), issued the Statutes of Rhuddlan, imposing English laws and administration on Wales

Flodden: in northern England, where in 1513 a Scottish army was defeated by the English; the King of Scots and many of his nobles were killed

Everybody suddenly burst out singing . . .: first three lines of Sassoon's poem 'Everyone Sang' (April 1919)

Chapter 26

Graves leaves the army, February 1919; he lives with his wife and child in Wales.

NOTES AND GLOSSARY:

Hove:	a town on the south coast of England
Jenny:	Jenny Nicholson (1919–64), who became an actress
Twelfth Night:	6 January, the twelfth day after Christmas
shillelaghs:	Irish wooden cudgels, named after a small town in County Wicklow in Ireland
Plymouth Brethren:	a very strict Protestant sect who deny themselves most of the pleasures of life
O'Connell Street:	re-named after Daniel O'Connell (1775–1847), Irish patriot
Georgian:	the architectural style of the time of King George III, who reigned from 1760 to 1820
Home Rule:	an Irish government independent of the British parliament in London was promised before the war, but delayed by it
Is there any song...:	these doggerel verses contain allusions to three nursery rhymes: 'Simple Simon', 'How many miles to Babylon?' and 'Ride a cock horse'
Some speak of Alexander:	the first lines of *The British Grenadiers* (see Chapter 11); the second word should read 'talk'
Alexander:	Alexander the Great (356–323BC), King of Macedon and conqueror of a vast, if short-lived, empire stretching from Egypt to India
Hercules:	the legendary Greek hero, famous for his strength and daring
Mods:	short for 'Moderations', undergraduate examinations at Oxford University
stumer:	(*slang*) worthless
Cinna in *Julius Caesar*:	a minor part in Shakespeare's play (1599)
Blackpool Pier:	a place of public entertainment at Blackpool, a popular seaside holiday resort on the north-west coast of England
'The Handcuff King':	that is, the man was an escapologist; Graves based his story 'You Win, Houdini' upon this character (see *The Shout and Other Stories*, pages 116–27)
the Shannon:	the longest river in Ireland; it flows through Limerick
the Troubles:	the violence and turmoil in Ireland before its independence
jaunting-car:	a small Irish horse-drawn vehicle
doubled:	ran
Fishguard:	a seaport in Wales
South Wales Echo:	a newspaper
Paddington:	a London railway station

Ealing: a western suburb of London

the whole bag of tricks: (*slang*) everything that is required

Brighton: a town on the south coast of England adjoining Hove

'The Troll's Nosegay': this poem still appears in Graves's *Collected Poems*

Shoreham Camp: a military barracks near Brighton

Philip Snowden: English Socialist politician (1864–1937), an opponent of the war who lost his seat in Parliament in the 1918 General Election

platform: the stated policies of a political candidate or party

Ramsay MacDonald: Labour politician (1866–1937), later British Prime Minister in 1924 and 1929–35; he had opposed the war

Dolwreiddiog Farm: a farm in the hills behind Harlech, in the valley of the river Artro

unbuttoning: undoing his trousers in order to urinate

I could not use a telephone: because of the incident mentioned in Chapter 10, page 65

Daily Herald: a national newspaper founded in 1912 to reflect the views of the Labour Party

the blockade of Russia: the Allies attempted to intervene in the civil war which broke out after the revolution in Russia, 1917

Paris: the real centre of the peace negotiations; Versailles is a palace outside Paris, where the treaty was signed

Hawker's Atlantic flight: in May, 1919, the Australian H. G. Hawker (1888–1921) and his navigator, Commander Grieve, tried to fly from Canada to Britain but fell in the sea; luckily they were picked up by a ship

Lady Diana Manners: the youngest daughter (*b*.1892) of the Duke of Rutland; on 2 June 1919 she married Alfred Duff Cooper (1890–1954), later Viscount Norwich, politician, diplomat and author

The Panther: although this horse was favourite to win the Derby, the leading English flat race, on 4 June 1919, it was unplaced; the winning horse was called Grand Parade

the mark: the unit of currency in Germany; in 1923 its buying-power fell to virtually nothing

Czarist: the emperor of Russia was known as the Czar or Tsar, a form of the name 'Caesar' used by Roman Emperors; compare the German equivalent 'Kaiser'

Constructive Birth Control Society: the Society for Constructive Birth Control and Racial Progress, founded in 1921 as a

	result of the work of the eugenicist Marie Stopes (1880–1958)
my publisher:	William Heinemann (1863–1920)

Chapter 27

Graves goes to Oxford as a student, but is tormented by war memories.

NOTES AND GLOSSARY:

Keble College:	one of the Oxford colleges, founded 1870
within the three-mile radius:	students were supposed to live within three miles of the university
Boar's Hill:	a place south-west of Oxford
the Proctor's bulldogs:	the Proctors are responsible for university discipline; their assistants are nicknamed 'bulldogs'
G. N. Clark:	Sir George Norman Clark (1890–1979), historian
Oriel:	another Oxford college, founded in 1326
Soviet:	the name for associations of soldiers and workers in Russia at the time of the 1917 revolution
Woodstock and Banbury Roads:	Oxford street names
Percy Simpson:	literary scholar (1865–1962); with C. H. Herford (1853–1931) he edited the plays of Ben Jonson (1572–1637) in 11 volumes (1925–52)
the Romantic Revivalists:	the writers and poets of the late eighteenth and early nineteenth centuries
Shelley:	Percy Bysshe Shelley (1792–1822), a leading English Romantic poet
Anglo-Saxon:	the language, now referred to as Old English, spoken and written in England in the centuries before the Norman Conquest, 1066, a French invasion
Beowulf:	the hero of the greatest Old English poem, an epic of about 3,000 lines
Gothland:	in southern Sweden, the scene of Beowulf's fight with a monster
Judith:	the heroine of a book in the Apocrypha (see note to Chapter 23) who kills an enemy general, Holofernes, in his tent; there is an Old English poem telling this story
***Brunanburgh*:**	an Old English battle poem
Edmund Blunden:	English poet and literary scholar (1896–1974); he served in the Royal Sussex regiment in the First World War and his memoirs, *Undertones of War* (1928), rank with Graves's and Sassoon's as records of the war

bullee beef: bully beef, that is, corned beef, a staple of British Army rations

'shun!: attention (army command)

like a shot: (*slang*) without hesitation

Robert Bridges: English poet (1844–1930), Poet Laureate, 1913–30

the Oxford recantation of war-time hatred: to restore academic links between Britain and Germany Bridges wrote a letter of reconciliation which was signed by over fifty Oxford scholars, including T. E. Lawrence; see *The Times*, 18 October 1920

Dr Gilbert Murray: Australian classical scholar and translator of ancient Greek plays (1866–1957)

the League of Nations: an international organisation for peace, 1920–46; the forerunner of the United Nations and even less successful

Aristotle's *Poetics*: a work on poetry and drama by the Greek philosopher Aristotle (384–322BC)

Browne: William Brown (1881–1952), Wilde Reader in Mental Philosophy at Oxford University, 1921–46

Reynard the Fox: published in 1919

Airedale: a breed of dog named after a valley in Yorkshire in northern England

bridge: a card game

halfpenny a hundred: the losers would pay the winners a halfpenny for every hundred points by which they lost the game; a very small gamble

Robert Nichols: English poet (1893–1944) whose war poems were at first much admired

Three Musketeers: the title of an historical adventure novel published in 1844 by the Frenchman Alexandre Dumas (1803–70)

David: David Graves (1920–43); see Epilogue

Chapter 28

Graves meets T. E. Lawrence and Thomas Hardy; Nancy starts a shop, which fails.

NOTES AND GLOSSARY:

All Souls: an Oxford college, founded in 1438

Fellowship: membership of a college at Oxford

Regius Professor of Divinity: Arthur Cayley Headlam (1862–1947), Regius Professor of Divinity at Oxford from 1918 to 1923, when he became Bishop of Gloucester

Gadara: a town near the southern shore of the Sea of Galilee,
                           now the ruins of Umm Qays
Lake of Galilee: the Sea of Galilee, between modern Israel and Syria
St James: one of Jesus's disciples, the author of an epistle or
                           letter in the Christian New Testament of the Bible
Mnasalcus: Greek poet (fourth century BC); he does not seem to
                           be quoted in the Epistle of St James
Meleager: Greek poet (*c*.140–70BC), born at Gadara
the Greek Anthology: a collection of poems in ancient Greek, including
                           some by Mnasalcus and Meleager, made in the tenth
                           century AD by Constantine Cephalos
a book of yours: probably either *Over the Brazier* (1916) or *Fairies
                           and Fusiliers* (1917)
the Peace Conference: the negotiations in Paris to end the war
Emir Feisal: King Feisal (1885–1933), king of Hejaz and, from
                           1921, Iraq
The Seven Pillars of Wisdom: Lawrence's war memoirs, first published
                           privately in 1926
the Arab Revolt: the rebellion of the Arabs against Turkish rule;
                           Britain encouraged this as part of the war
audit ale: especially strong ale
barley water: a drink made by boiling barley in water
Prince Albert of Schleswig-Holstein: Albert John Charles Frederick
                           Alfred George, Duke of Schleswig-Holstein (1869–
                           1931), a grandson of Queen Victoria
Lowell Thomas: American writer, broadcaster and film-maker
                           (*b*.1892); from 1919 he travelled worldwide giving
                           his lecture 'With Lawrence in Arabia' and published
                           a book with this title in 1924
Thomas Hardy: English poet and novelist (1840–1928); see later in
                           this chapter
Charles Doughty: English writer and traveller (1843–1926); one of the
                           first Europeans to travel in the Arab world
Hogarth: David Hogarth (1862–1927), English archaeologist
                           and biographer of Doughty
Ashmolean Museum: a museum of antiquities and art treasures at
                           Oxford, begun from the collections of Elias
                           Ashmole (1617–92)
Spenser: Edmund Spenser (?1552–99), English poet
Vachel Lindsay: American poet (1879–1931)
Middle-Western: from the mid-western states of the U.S.A.
Sir Walter Raleigh: English literary critic (1861–1922)
Illinois Anti-Saloon League: a temperance society in the state of Illinois,
                           U.S.A.

King Charles:	Charles I, king of England 1625–49; many churches and other institutions gave their gold and silver treasures to finance his war against Parliament
Augustus John:	English painter (1878–1961)
a Kelmscott *Chaucer*:	an edition of the poetry of Geoffrey Chaucer (?1345–1400) produced by the Kelmscott Press, started in 1890 by the English poet and craftsman William Morris (1834–96)
Tell Shawm:	Tell esh Shahim, a railway station on the Hejaz Railway, taken by the British, 12 April 1917
Hedjaz Railway:	the Hejaz Railway was built by the Turks south from Damascus in Syria and then south-east through the Hejaz, the region on the eastern shore of the Red Sea, to Medina; it was repeatedly attacked, by Lawrence and others, throughout 1917
Carchemish:	an ancient city on the upper Euphrates river, a centre of the Hittite civilisation of around 1000BC; Lawrence assisted in the excavation of the site before the war
***The Pierglass*:**	published in 1921
Radcliffe Camera:	a circular eighteenth-century building at Oxford, named after John Radcliffe (1650–1714), a royal physician
Jesus College:	an Oxford college, founded in 1571
the Quadrangle:	the courtyard enclosed by the college buildings
Winston Churchill:	English statesman (1874–1965), British Prime Minister, 1940–5, during the Second World War, and 1951–5; he was Secretary of State for the Colonies, 1921–2
the Middle-Eastern settlement of 1922:	the settlement referred to was reached at the Cairo Conference of 1921, not 1922
Magdalen College:	another Oxford college, founded 1458
Lord Curzon:	George Nathaniel Curzon, Marquess of Kedleston (1859–1925), Viceroy of India, 1899–1905, and Foreign Secretary, 1918–22; he was Chancellor, not Vice-Chancellor, of Oxford University from 1907
Ezra Pound:	American poet and critic (1885–1972), a leader of the modernist movement in English literature
Sir William Orpen:	Irish-born painter (1878–1931); a war-artist, 1917–18
Professor Edgeworth:	Francis Edgeworth (1845–1926), Professor of Political Economy at Oxford from 1891
caliginous:	misty, foggy
Metropolis:	the city, that is, London

inspissated: dense, thick

Fuller's Tea Shop: there were several of these in England, including one in the Cornmarket, Oxford; it closed twenty years ago

a Government Blue-book: an official government report, so-called from the colour of its cover

Stationery Office: the government printing house and bookseller

a Royal Commission: an official government investigation of a specific problem

Balliol and Queen's: two more Oxford colleges, founded in 1263 and 1340

the long vacation: there is no teaching at British universities between July and October

Devon: a county in the south-west of England

Salisbury Plain: in the south-western county of Wiltshire; part of it is still used for military training

Stonehenge: a circle of massive stone blocks erected on Salisbury Plain in prehistoric times, probably for a religious purpose to do with astronomical events

Dorchester: a town in Dorset, a county on the south coast of England

his honorary doctor's degree: given to Hardy at a ceremony on 10 January 1920

the Red Terror: atrocities committed by the Communists or Reds against the monarchists or Whites in the Russian Civil War, 1917–20

his old work: Hardy was the son of a builder and had been trained as an architect and stonemason

Wessex: the name Hardy applied to the area of south-west England where his novels are set

***Tess of the D'Urbervilles*:** one of Hardy's novels, published in 1891

Athenaeum Club: a London gentleman's club

Henry James: American novelist (1843–1916); he became a British citizen in 1915

***Message to the American People*:** this work cannot be identified; perhaps Hardy never completed it

Swanage: a small town on the south coast of England, not far from Dorchester

'this shape smalled in the distance': this line remains unidentified, but Hardy used the word 'small' as a verb in three poems: 'Departure' (1901), 'The Dead Quire' (1909) and 'The Shiver' (1925)

Lawrence: that is, T. E. Lawrence; see his letter to Graves of 8 September 1923

Homer's *Iliad*:	the *Iliad* is an epic poem by the Greek poet Homer (perhaps tenth century BC)
***Marmion*:**	a narrative poem by Sir Walter Scott (1771–1832), whose once high reputation had declined considerably by the 1920s
***vers libre*:**	(*French*) 'free verse'; verse not written in stanzas or strict metre, the form of much modernist verse, for example, that of T. S. Eliot
Anti-Profiteering Committee:	as a Justice of the Peace (a civilian magistrate) in Dorchester, Hardy was involved in trying food-profiteering cases, 1917–19, but did not serve on a special committee
in a ring:	had an agreement to maintain high prices
The *Daily Mirror*:	a national newspaper
Parnassus:	a mountain in Greece sacred to the spirit of poetry
Sir Arthur Evans:	British archaeologist (1851–1941), famous for his discovery of the ancient civilisation of Crete, a Mediterranean island
Wootton:	a village south-west of Oxford, near Boar's Hill
Robin Hood:	the legendary English outlaw who was said to rob the rich to pay the poor
a quarter:	a quarter of a pound
a beamed attic:	a room under the roof where the roof-timbers are exposed
ordnance map:	an Ordnance Survey map, part of a series, originally drawn for military purposes in the early nineteenth century, covering the whole of Britain
Islip:	a village north of Oxford

Chapter 29

Graves and his family settle at Islip, near Oxford, 1921.

NOTES AND GLOSSARY:

Constable:	the local policeman
centre-forward . . . inside-left:	team positions in association football
dribbling:	running along controlling the ball with the feet
Love in a cottage:	a married life filled with affection rather than material comfort
my prose books:	between 1921 and 1925, Graves published *On English Poetry* (1922), *The Meaning of Dreams* (1925) and *Poetic Unreason and Other Studies* (1925)
railway warrant:	a special pass to allow free travel on the railway
Chipping Norton:	a town about twenty miles north-west of Oxford

workhouse:	institutions for the maintenance of the poor and unemployed
service:	work as a household servant
the baby class:	the youngest class, about five years old, just learning to read and write
ast:	(*dialect*) ask
'Course:	of course
Spikes:	(*slang*) workhouses
mug:	(*slang*) face
cop:	(*slang*) policeman
bums:	(*slang*) vagrants and down-and-outs
carbolic:	a disinfectant
squitch:	couch-grass (*Triticum repens*), a common weed
parish council:	governing body for a small area of England, dealing with local affairs
District Council:	governing body with a slightly larger responsibility than a parish council

this time with no 'Evils of Alcoholism': see Chapter 16, page 150

bridle-path:	path for horseriders
the Rector:	the local clergyman
Tower of Siloam:	in the Bible, Jesus asks: 'Or those eighteen, upon whom the tower in Siloam fell, and slew them, think ye that they were sinners above all men that dwelt in Jerusalem?' (Luke 13:4)
the Cherwell:	the river which flows through Oxford

the siege of Oxford: Oxford was King Charles I's headquarters during the Civil War and was besieged in 1645

cavalry skirmish at Islip bridge: this occurred on 23 May 1645

Westminster Abbey: founded in the seventh or eighth century AD and much enlarged by Edward the Confessor, king of England, 1042–66; it is now surrounded by the buildings of London

the Norman Conquest: in 1066 Duke William of Normandy (?1027–87) invaded England from France and became king

---

Chapter 30

Graves's literary career, 1920–25.

NOTES AND GLOSSARY:

B.A.:	Bachelor of Arts

the official history of the war in the air: Sir Walter Raleigh wrote the first volume, published in 1922

R.A.F.:	Royal Air Force

The Illogical Element in English Poetry: published as *Poetic Unreason*, 1925

a volume of poetry every year: *Country Sentiment* (1920), *The Pierglass* (1921), *Whipperginny* (1922), *The Feather Bed* (1923), *Mock Beggar Hall* (1924) and *Welchman's Hose* (1925)

Walter de la Mare: English poet (1873–1956)

W. H. Davies: English poet and autobiographical writer (1871–1940)

T. S. Eliot: American poet (1888–1965) who settled in England, where for a time he worked in a bank

the Sitwells: Osbert and Sacheverell (see Chapter 23) and their sister Edith (1887–1964), a poet

Ah, no man knows . . .: from de la Mare's poem 'All That's Past'

Renishaw: the Sitwells' ancestral home, in Derbyshire, a county in the Midlands of England

***avant garde*:** (*French*) in the forefront of artistic innovation

Professor of English Literature to Tokyo: Blunden held this post from 1924 to 1927

Lawrence enlisted in the R.A.F.: in a confused attempt to escape his fame, T. E. Lawrence joined the R.A.F. in 1922 under the name John Hume Ross, but the newspapers (not, as Graves says, a member of parliament) discovered this and he was forced to leave. Instead, as T. E. Shaw, he joined the Royal Tank Corps in 1923, but he disliked the army and two years later transferred back to the R.A.F., where he remained for ten years; during that time questions were asked about him in Parliament, but he was not again forced to leave

Lord Lloyd: George Ambrose Lloyd, Baron Lloyd (1879–1941), High Commissioner for Egypt, 1925–9

Colonel John Buchan: Scottish novelist (1875–1940); he had a house at Elsfield Manor, near Oxford

---

Chapter 31

Graves goes to Egypt as Professor of English Literature at Cairo, 1926.

NOTES AND GLOSSARY:

P. & O.: the Peninsular and Oriental Steam Navigation Company, a passenger shipping line

Morris-Oxford: a British-built motor car

Lafcadio Hearn: traveller and author (1850–1904); he spent seven years as a lecturer on English Literature in Japan

Nichols: Robert Nichols (see Chapter 27, page 241) was Professor of English at Tokyo University, 1921–4

Wilfred Jennings Bramly: no further information discovered

Groppi's: a café in Cairo, famous for its sweet pastries and favoured by European residents; it still exists

in the image of our Maker: the Bible says 'God created man in his own image' (Genesis 1:27)

Stromboli: an island volcano in the Mediterranean Sea between Italy and Sicily

Port Said: a port on the Mediterranean coast of Egypt, at the head of the Suez Canal

Kipling's 'wattles of Lichtenburg': a reference to Kipling's poem 'Lichtenberg (New South Wales Contingent)', which is about Australia

Gizereh: El Gezira, an island in the Nile, full of costly houses occupied in Graves's time by Europeans and rich Egyptians

Heliopolis: a modern suburb to the east of Cairo, a mile or so south-east of the site of ancient Heliopolis, of which only ruins and the obelisk of Sesostris I (1971–28BC) remain

King Fuad: Fu'ad (1868–1936), King of Egypt

Mohammed: the founder of the Moslem religion (c. AD570–632)

Khedive: the title of the Turkish governor of Egypt in the latter nineteenth century

Zaghlul Pasha: Ahmad Sa'd Zaghlul (1860–1927), Egyptian nationalist political leader

Byron: George Gordon, Lord Byron (1788–1824), Romantic poet

King David: the second king of Israel, reputed to be the author of the poems contained in the Book of Psalms of the Bible

the Sphinx: Graves probably means the gigantic representation of this fabulous creature, half-lion, half-human, near the Great Pyramid of Giza

fellaheen: Egyptian peasants

Oxford bags: trousers with extremely wide legs, a fashion craze of the 1920s

Ramadan: the ninth month of the Moslem year, during which the faithful fast from dawn to sunset

the Koran: the holy book of Islam, the Moslem religious faith

Jesuit college: the Society of Jesus, founded in 1534, is a Roman Catholic missionary organisation which wins converts by setting up schools in non-Christian lands

Maison Cicurel: a European-style department store in Cairo; it still exists

Pallas: one of the names of the ancient Greek goddess of wisdom, industry and war

Aphrodite: the ancient Greek goddess of love and beauty

Artemis: the ancient Greek goddess of the moon, chastity and hunting

American College: the American University in*central Cairo

piastres: the piastre is the smallest unit of currency in Egypt

Buddha: the title, meaning 'enlightened' or 'wise', given to the founder of one of the chief religions of eastern Asia

Voltaire: the name taken by François Marie Arouet (1694–1778), French poet, historian and philosopher

Rousseau: Jean-Jacques Rousseau (1712–78), French writer on society and education

Samuel Smiles's *Self Help*: Samuel Smiles (1812–1904), Scottish biographer and social reformer, published *Self-Help* in 1859

since the eighties: Britain took over Egypt in 1882, displacing a French influence dating back to Napoleon's invasion of 1798

the dagoes: a derogatory name for certain Mediterranean peoples, here presumably the Italians, given their influence over King Fu'ad (see Chapter 32, page 276)

El Azhar: al Azhar, a mosque in central Cairo, founded AD972, a centre of Islamic theology for centuries and now a university

Judge Preston: no further information discovered

Turf Club: a favourite European club in Cairo

a parthenogenous birth: a virgin birth

Chapter 32

Egyptian experiences. Graves returns to England; his marriage to Nancy ends, 1929.

NOTES AND GLOSSARY:

Mahmoud Mohammed Mahmoud: this and the other two essayists' names were surely invented by Graves

Darwin: Charles Darwin (1809–82), English biologist, whose theory of evolution assumed a process of gradual, not violent, change in the history of the earth

mamel: mistake for 'breast' (from the French 'mamelle')

draught: mistake for 'drought'

fatigable: easily tired (from a French word of similar meaning)

Freubel: Friedrich Froebel (1782–1852), German educationist, inventor of the kindergarten for pre-school education

Lady Macbeth: the wife of the hero of Shakespeare's tragedy *Macbeth* (1605–6); the essay is a rough paraphrase of the latter part of Act I Scene 7 of the play

ascuse: mistake for 'accuse' (confused with its opposite 'excuse')

to lay: mistake for 'to give birth to'

'All work and no play . . .: an English proverb

gumbling: mistake for 'gambling'

leavy: mistake for 'leafy'

lasy: mistake for 'lazy'

Gray's *Elegy*: *Elegy Written in a Country Churchyard* (1750), a poem by Thomas Gray (1716–71)

dues: mistake for 'dews'

sweat: mistake for 'sweet'

'reading maketh a full man': from the essay 'Of Studies' by Francis Bacon (1561–1626)

'Every schoolboy knows': a phrase associated with the English writer Lord Macaulay (1800–59), though earlier examples of its use can be found

The whale came . . . to carry the Greek musician . . .: an allusion to a Greek myth; when Arion, a legendary musician, was thrown overboard, he was brought to land by a dolphin which had earlier been charmed by his singing

hold a mirror up to nature: from Act III Scene 2 of Shakespeare's *Hamlet* (1600–1), referring to acting, not music

widdening: mistake for 'widening'

a sound mind . . . in a sound body: the ancient Roman ideal of physical and mental health, 'mens sana in corpore sano' (*Latin*)

the Egyptian Exhibition: presumably the display of Egyptian antiquities in the Cairo museum

Milton: John Milton (1608–74), English poet; the allusion is to his poem 'Il Penseroso' (1632)

Addison: Joseph Addison (1672–1719), English essayist

Palmerstone: Henry John Temple, Viscount Palmerston (1784–1865), British statesman and Prime Minister, 1855–65

Sudanese: the Sudan, the country south of Egypt, had been conquered by the Egyptians, 1820–2; from 1898 to 1956 it was ruled jointly by Britain and Egypt

the Khamsin: a hot south or south-easterly wind which blows in Egypt during March, April and May

Lars Porsena . . .: published in 1927, revised edition, 1936; the title alludes to the opening lines of 'Horatius', the first of the *Lays of Ancient Rome* (1842) by Lord Macaulay: 'Lars Porsena of Clusium/By the Nine Gods he swore . . .'

Pharaoh Seti the Good: Seti I, who ruled Egypt in the fourteenth century BC; his mummy was found in 1886

A.D.C.: (*French*) 'aide-de-camp', an officer in attendance upon a general

Union Jack: the British flag

Sir Lee Stack: English general (1868–1924), Sirdar or commander of the Egyptian army from 1917 until his murder in Cairo

Abdin Palace: the royal palace in Cairo, begun in 1863

morning coat: a formal black coat

opera hats: black top hats

shot up by an assassin: an assassination attempt was indeed made on Fu'ad, but in 1898, when he was thirty years old

soirée: (*French*) 'evening entertainment'

Arabian Nights: *The Arabian Nights Entertainments* or *The Thousand and One Nights*, a collection of fabulous stories from Arabia, Persia, Egypt and India

Venice: a city in Italy, on the northern shore of the Adriatic Sea

Inoui: (*French*) 'unheard of, extraordinary'

Cheops: king of Egypt around 2650BC

Chawki Bey: Ahmad Shawqi (1868–1932), one of Egypt's foremost poets and playwrights

Moorish: in the style of the Moors, the people of north-west Africa

the Nile: the great river which flows through Egypt

Joseph: in the Bible (Genesis 41), the Hebrew Joseph interprets the Egyptian Pharoah's dream as a prophecy of famine and so food-stocks are prepared

New characters appeared: in fact, Graves met Laura Riding (*b.*1901), the American poet who was to dominate his life until 1939, before he left for Egypt and she had gone to Cairo, too

Epilogue

Graves sketches his life from 1929 to 1957.

NOTES AND GLOSSARY:

Spanish Civil War: this lasted from 1936 to 1939
the Second World War: this lasted from 1939 to 1945
W.A.A.F.: Women's Auxiliary Air Force
General Le Clerc: General Jacques Philippe Leclerc (*b.*1902), commander of the 2nd French Armoured Division, which took Paris, August 1944
General Adair: Major-General Sir Allan Adair (*b.*1897), commander of the British Guards Armoured Division, 1942–5
Arnhem: a town in Holland; in September 1944 British paratroops landed there but were defeated by the Germans before help could reach them
Clifford Dalton: he died in 1961
Calais: a French port on the English Channel, taken by the Germans, May 1940
Madagascar: a large island off the east coast of Africa, once a French colony; after the surrender of France to Germany in 1940 Britain invaded it to prevent its use as a German naval base
Arakan peninsula: in Burma, then a British colony, which was invaded by Japan in 1942
His Majesty: George VI, king of Britain, 1936–52
Sergeant Roger Lamb: subject of two books by Graves, *Sergeant Lamb of the Ninth* (1940) and *Proceed, Sergeant Lamb* (1941)
John Milton's behaviour: described in Graves's book *The Story of Mary Powell: Wife to Mr Milton* (1943)
especial constabulary: a police reserve force
Heil Hitler!: (*German*) 'Hail Hitler!'; Adolf Hitler (1889–1945) was the leader of Germany in the Second World War
Air Raid Warden: a part-time volunteer who supervised precautions against aerial bombing
Exeter: the main town in the county of Devon
eventually got divorced: on 18 November 1949
I married again: on 11 May 1950 Graves married Beryl Pritchard (*b.*1915), who had once been married to Graves's friend Alan Hodge (1915–79)
four more children: William (*b.*1940), Lucia (*b.*1943), Juan (*b.*1944) and Tomas (*b.*1953)

Prince Charles: the eldest son (*b*.1948) of the present ruler of Britain, Queen Elizabeth II; in fact he went to Gordonstoun, a school in Scotland

Vaughan-Williams: Ralph Vaughan-Williams (1872–1958), British composer

O.M.: Order of Merit

the *Carmen Carthusianum*: (*Latin*) the Charterhouse Song

Palma: the main town of Majorca

Lester Pearson: Canadian statesman (1897–1972), Prime Minister of Canada, 1963–8

Malcolm Muggeridge: English writer and television personality (*b*.1903); he was a lecturer at Cairo University, 1927–30, and edited the humorous magazine *Punch*, 1953–7

Colonel Nasser: Gamal Abdel Nasser (1918–70), President of Egypt, 1956–70; it is hard to believe he was taught by Graves in 1926

Prince Charles's great-great-great-grandmother: Queen Victoria

Appendix

British Infantry Regiments mentioned in *Goodbye to All That*, in order of seniority

Grenadier Guards: the senior regiment of Foot Guards, dating back to 1656

Irish Guards: the fourth regiment of Foot Guards, raised in 1900

Welsh Guards: the fifth and youngest of the Foot Guards, raised in 1915

Queen's Royal Regiment: first raised in 1661; a London regiment

King's Own Royal Lancaster Regiment: raised in 1680; Lancaster is the county town of Lancashire, in northern England

Northumberland Fusiliers: raised in 1674; Northumberland is a county in north-east England

Royal Warwickshire Regiment: raised in 1673; Warwickshire is in the Midlands of England

Royal Fusiliers: raised in 1685; a London regiment

Suffolk Regiment: raised in 1685; Suffolk is in eastern England

Bedfordshire Regiment: raised in 1688; Bedfordshire is a county forty miles north of London. Most of its service was in the Americas and so it missed the major European wars and battle honours

Green Howards: raised in 1688; a regiment from Yorkshire, in the north of England

Cheshire Regiment: raised in 1689; Cheshire is in the West Midlands of England, near Wales. Most of its service was in America and India before 1914

Royal Welsh Fusiliers: raised 1688; for more details, see Chapter 11. Not until 1920 was the spelling 'Welch' officially allowed

South Wales Borderers: raised in 1689

King's Own Scottish Borderers: raised in 1689, as the Edinburgh Regiment, and still has connections with the Scottish capital

Cameronians (Scottish Rifles): a combination of two Scottish regiments, the Cameronians, raised 1689, and the Perthshire Light Infantry, raised 1794

Gloucestershire Regiment: an English regiment, whose men wear a badge on both the front and back of their caps because at the Battle of Alexandria, 1801, they beat off simultaneous French attacks from front and rear

East Surrey Regiment: a regiment identified with the region just south of London

Border Regiment: from the English counties bordering Scotland

Hampshire Regiment: a regiment from the south coast of England

South Staffordshire Regiment: Staffordshire is a county in the industrial Midlands of England

Welsh Regiment: a combination of two battalions, the 41st, formed from invalid companies raised in 1719 but in 1822 called the Welsh Regiment, and the 69th South Lincolnshires, an English regiment; both served mainly outside Europe before 1914

Black Watch (Royal Highlanders): the oldest regiment of kilted Scottish Highlanders, raised in 1725

Oxfordshire and Buckinghamshire Light Infantry: a combination of two regiments from neighbouring counties west of London

King's Own Yorkshire Light Infantry: another regiment from the north of England

Middlesex Regiment: a London regiment, known as 'The Diehards' because, at the battle of Albuera in Spain, 1811, their wounded colonel called on his men to 'die hard'

Wiltshire Regiment: a south-west English regiment

Manchester Regiment: a regiment belonging to the West Midlands city

North Staffordshire Regiment: another English Midlands regiment

Highland Light Infantry: a Scottish regiment, although as light infantry they wore trousers, not the kilt

Gordon Highlanders: a kilted Scottish Highland regiment
Queen's Own Cameron Highlanders: a kilted Scottish Highland regiment
Royal Irish Rifles: a regiment from Northern Ireland
Connaught Rangers: an Irish regiment, disbanded in 1922
Argyll and Sutherland Highlanders: a kilted Scottish Highland regiment
Royal Munster Fusiliers: an Irish regiment, disbanded in 1922
The Rifle Brigade: formed in 1800, as an experiment with rifles rather than muskets, this became a regiment of several battalions of light infantry

Part 3

Commentary

Structure

Goodbye to All That is arranged in three parts. The first, Chapters 1 to 9, covers Graves's childhood and schooling. Graves does three things in this section. First, he gives a picture of life in Europe before the First World War, with particular emphasis on its morals, its class divisions and the family as an institution. Second, he shows his own gradual estrangement from this world and its values, especially in his account of his troubled time at Charterhouse School. Third, in a variety of ways, he expresses the threat of the war to come. Sometimes this is done by a jarring aside, as when he says of his cousin Wilhelm in Chapter 4 that he was 'later shot down in an air battle by a school-fellow of mine' (page 27); more generally it is done by unstated irony, for instance, by Graves's listing his German ancestry so prominently in Chapter 1.

The second section, Chapters 10 to 25, of *Goodbye to All That* is the longest and deals, of course, with the First World War. Here Graves makes bitter use of irony, contrasting life in England with conditions at the war front, the army commanders' hopeful plans with the hopeless confusion of infantry battles and the inhumanity of war with the individuality of the men he meets in France. These paradoxes reach a climax in Chapter 24, when Graves, attempting to prevent Sassoon's court-martial for his protest against the war, exclaims 'The irony of having to argue to these mad old men that Siegfried was not sane!' (page 216). In general, then, Graves shows how the war overturned the values of pre-war life, its genteel civilisation and its respect for authority.

The third section of the book, Chapters 26 to 32, though it seems an anti-climax and is certainly more confused, is essential as a picture of the aftermath of the war. Graves continues to contrast official and institutional attitudes with those of the individual, usually himself, first at Oxford University, then at Cairo. The older generation has complacently returned to its old assumptions, but the younger men who have survived the war are now less inclined to be deferential. Haunted by their terrible experiences, they become, like Graves, critical of society and increasingly estranged from it, and they align themselves, not with the leaders of the country they were trained to succeed, but with the underprivileged – the poor, the unemployed and the uneducated.

Characters

In all three parts of *Goodbye to All That* Graves makes use of certain people so that it is permissible to talk of his characterisation of them. Since he uses these characters for very much the same purpose throughout it is perhaps true to say they are all given the same character. In the end this is seen to be much the same as the character Graves wishes to give himself, with the difference that Graves presents himself as an anti-hero. The various caricature scenes emphasised in the book, as, for instance, his wedding, with 'Nancy savagely muttering the responses, myself shouting them in a parade-ground voice' (Chapter 25, page 223), prevent us from regarding Graves himself as a hero. Nevertheless, there are heroes in the book, and their heroism, for Graves, consists in their individuality, asserted against official disapproval. Inevitably, this leads to difficulties, so that Graves's characters appear not just as heroes but often also as victims.

The first of these hero-victims is Raymond Rodakowski, the friend Graves makes at Charterhouse in Chapter 7. He, like Graves, is a misfit at the school, studious, cultured and victimised because of his parentage. He encourages Graves's interest in poetry, but rather scandalises him by his religious unorthodoxy. Later, of course, Graves will come to reject Christianity, too. One function of these hero figures in *Goodbye to All That* is to express unconventional ideas with which Graves quietly agrees; thus he himself appears a less eccentric figure.

The next of Graves's heroes is George Mallory the mountaineer, not just because of his climbing achievements (which give Graves the opportunity to boast of his), but also because he too is at odds with authority, a misfit at Charterhouse who 'tried to treat his class in a friendly way' (page 56). This anticipates Graves's own attempts to be a humane leader of his men as an army officer.

The prominence given to these two figures early in *Goodbye to All That* sets a pattern for the rest. The chief example, however, occurs in the second section, about the war. Among the many heroic victims Graves mentions in this section one stands out: Siegfried Sassoon. Again Graves uses a character to state ideas he obviously agrees with but hesitates to make completely his own. Instead, it is Sassoon's protest against the war that he stresses, making it more poignant by the earlier portrait of Sassoon as idealistic and enthusiastic. He then casts Sassoon as the victim of his own good intentions, extricated only when Graves makes on his behalf a compromise with the army's debased values.

In the last section of the book Graves extends his technique to two famous figures. The first is T. E. Lawrence, whose portrait in Chapter 28 expresses both the unfittedness of ex-soldiers for life after the war and their justified contempt for empty conventions. It is clear that Graves relishes Lawrence's outrageous behaviour, although he presents himself as a demure onlooker. When Lawrence rings a station bell from his college window at Oxford, Graves mildly protests, yet clearly agrees with Lawrence's assertion that the place needs waking up.

The second famous person Graves uses as a hero is Thomas Hardy. Again, Hardy is made to seem even more unconventional in some ways than Graves, for example, in his comment on Nancy's refusal to call herself Nancy Graves: 'Why, you *are* old-fashioned!' (page 248). He also voices opinions Graves shares, especially about poetry and critics; the whole portrait seems an attempt by Graves to make Hardy a model for himself as a poet, just as he uses Raymond Rodakowski, George Mallory, Siegfried Sassoon and T. E. Lawrence as models or reflections of himself at various stages in his life.

Biographers of Thomas Hardy have dismissed Graves's picture of him as inaccurate and Sassoon was so annoyed by *Goodbye to All That* that he broke off his friendship with Graves. Both reactions suggest how far Graves is using these real-life figures as characters for his own ends. By comparison Graves himself appears from *Goodbye to All That* as a man whose orthodox ideas were slowly revised by circumstances and contact with bolder thinkers, and even then he was more restrained. The implication is that if even an ordinary person like Graves could come to share such unconventional views, then radical changes must have taken place during the thirty years described in the book.

Style

Two aspects of the style of *Goodbye to All That* are worth discussing and both are aspects of its unconventionality. The first is the variety of kinds of writing Graves employs, or perhaps we should say includes, because not all of the writing is his own. An amazing number of literary forms appear in the book: verses, songs, letters, military orders, essays, drama (as in Chapter 10), newspaper articles and, according to the opening of Chapter 12, 'reconstituted' novel. Such variety not only offends against conventional notions of stylistic unity, it also suggests disorder and a breakdown of rules and conventions, reflecting the theme of the book itself.

Another effect is to make us question the credibility of what we read. Graves often quotes what seem to be true statements which he then shows are false. The most heartfelt passage in the book seems to be the 'Little Mother's' letter in Chapter 21, but its version of the war is quite different from Graves's first-hand evidence; and, similarly, Graves's colonel's letter to his mother in the previous chapter, however sincere, is mistaken, because Graves is not dead, only wounded. On the other hand, Graves himself recounts as fact many amazing tales, sometimes sensationally, sometimes humorously. He delights in the odd and the extraordinary, daring us to disbelieve him. He introduces the reader to a world where plain statements, like the report of his death in *The Times*, are probably false and where far-fetched claims, such as that the gas-company's spanners were the wrong size to open the cylinders (Chapter 15, page 128), are probably true.

The question of what is credible and what is not leads to a consideration of Graves's own writing style. In the prologue of 1957 he describes this as 'excusably ragged', presumably because he wrote the book very quickly and did not revise it carefully. Stylistic roughness is certainly common in *Goodbye to All That*, usually in the form of straggling sentences like this one from page 141: 'The men seemed in high spirits, even the survivors of the show: singing to the accompaniment of an accordion and a penny-whistle.' Graves makes frequent use of the colon or semi-colon to add a loose extension to a sentence. He also uses many colloquialisms, as in this sentence: 'We did a lot of work on our wire' (page 114); or this: 'Poetry and Dick were still almost all that really mattered' (page 51), in which the imprecision is very informal. He also frequently omits words, especially verbs, as in the following sentence: 'This, in spite of having lost a leg with a Red Cross unit on the Italian front' (page 57). Such omissions are sometimes confusing, as in this example: 'Three men got killed in these attempts; two officers and two men, wounded' (page 133). More generally, Graves appears very informal because of his frequent use of slang words and the high proportion of dialogue in his writing, which is reproduced with much colloquialism and often the suggestion of accent or dialect. This spoken quality even affects the non-dialogue prose, too, as on page 206, where Graves writes 'And who else? John Galsworthy; or did I first meet him a year or two later?', which sounds as though he is talking to the reader, or himself.

Graves's style, however, can be defended and even justified. It is difficult to write smoothly and include as much detail as Graves tries to. Much of the jerkiness of the style comes from the need to name people and places and explain their significance to the reader. At other points, an irregular prose rhythm has descriptive value, as in this sentence from page 110: 'We went ten yards at a time, slowly, not on all fours, but wriggling flat along the ground.' This descriptive justification applies particularly to the battle scenes and the accounts of trench warfare.

The virtue of Graves's ragged prose is that it seems consistent with the raw experiences he is narrating. Whether intentionally or not, he tries to convey an immediate impression of events by writing without elegance and smoothness, implying that he is giving his direct memories of his life, unmodified by literary polishing. It was probably wise of him, then, not to try to alter the style of *Goodbye to All That* when he revised it in

1957. The raggedness of Graves's prose, though unconventional, encourages the reader to believe what Graves has to say.

Ambiguity

Goodbye to All That is more than a book of war memoirs, as its title implies. Graves calls up his memories of three phases of his life and all they stand for in order to dismiss them in favour of a new existence, which he describes in the epilogue as not of 'outstanding autobiographical interest'; he was saying goodbye in 1929 to the notion of autobiography itself, which is why at times he mocks the form in *Goodbye to All That*.

Yet Graves's outlook appears more absolute than it is. He is never quite as tough and uncompromising as he would like the reader to believe. In all three sections of the book he reveals more affection for what he claims to be rejecting than perhaps he realises. The first part displays great pride in his ancestors and a respect for his parents, especially his mother, which outlasts his rejection of their morality and religion. The second part contains the paradox of Graves's attitude to the army; he spares the reader nothing of the horror and misery of war, but he also devotes a chapter to the glorious traditions of his regiment, the Royal Welch Fusiliers. In Chapter 17, he tells the frightening story of the officer who had, on two occasions, to shoot one of his own men in order to force the rest to attack the enemy; yet Graves's reaction is not pity for the men, but for the officer, saying: 'He deserved a better regiment' (page 155). In effect, Graves, like Sassoon, accepts the military virtues of courage, loyalty and honour while protesting against the war. In the last section something similar is evident. Graves turns against university life, as student and as professor, but really in the name of academic virtue. It is because he has strong feelings about literature that he is dissatisfied with the teaching at Oxford, and it is because he can do so little honest work that he resigns from Cairo University.

Goodbye to All That is therefore a rather ambivalent book. It records in minute detail what its author wants only to reject. It is written in a hurried style, yet, as these notes prove, is remarkably accurate about the hundreds of names and places mentioned. Finally, its fundamental values are much less unconventional than Graves would have us think.

Part 4

Hints for study

After you have read *Goodbye to All That*

A leading question you are bound to ask about *Goodbye to All That* is whether it is true. Does Graves give an accurate account, in particular, of trench warfare in the First World War? Graves himself has written, with his usual sense of mischief, that 'the memoirs of a man who went through some of the worst experiences of trench-warfare are not truthful if they do not contain a high proportion of falsities. High-explosive barrages will make a temporary liar or visionary of anyone . . .' To begin checking Graves's accuracy, read some of the books on the war mentioned in the 'Suggestions for further reading' in Part 5 of this book.

It is worth comparing Graves's autobiography with others of the time, again to check his accuracy and also to see how he chooses to deal with his material. The best insight into Graves's style and method is gained from comparison with what other writers have done in similar works. The most obvious book to compare with *Goodbye to All That* is Siegfried Sassoon's *Memoirs of an Infantry Officer* (1930), because Sassoon served in the same regiment and shared several experiences with Graves himself. Here, from Part IV, section 5, of his book is Sassoon's description of Graves (whom he calls 'David Cromlech'; one obvious difference between the books is Sassoon's use of pseudonyms):

> . . . no one was worse than he was at hitting it off with officers who distrusted cleverness and disliked unreserved utterances. In fact he was a positive expert at putting people's backs up unintentionally. He was with our Second Battalion for a few months before they transferred him to 'the First', and during that period the Colonel was heard to remark that young Cromlech threw his tongue a hell of a lot too much, and that it was about time he gave up reading Shakespeare and took to using soap and water. He had, however, added, 'I'm agreeably surprised to find that he isn't windy in trenches.'
>
> David certainly was deplorably untidy, and his absentmindedness when off duty was another propensity which made him unpopular . . .

How far does this agree with the impression we get of Graves from his own book? Is Sassoon being fair here, do you think, or is he exaggerating Graves's unpopularity, perhaps for his own purposes? Do you think Sassoon agrees with what the Colonel is supposed to have said about

Graves? Sassoon's style, like Graves's, is informal, with many colloquialisms ('hitting it off', 'putting people's backs up', 'a hell of a lot'), but it also contains here a certain archness or literary posing (in the phrase 'another propensity which made him unpopular') which hints at detachment and control. Sassoon, even in this brief extract, shapes his memories just as Graves does and probably uses Graves as a character just as Graves uses him in *Goodbye to All That*.

Another valuable comparison is with Edmund Blunden's *Undertones of War* (1928). Here for instance is Blunden describing a bombardment:

> ... as Limbery-Buse and myself sat in a dugout about as large but hardly as strong as a cabin trunk, amusing ourselves with very light literature and local satire, salvoes of whizzbangs gouged up the ground and splintered the duckboards two or three steps from our 'door'. This went on much too long ...   (Chapter 5)

Compare Graves's account of shelling in Chapter 20 of *Goodbye to All That*:

> ... shells bracketed along the trench about five yards short and five yards over, but never quite got it. Three times running, my cup of tea was spilled by the concussion and filled with dirt. I happened to be in a cheerful mood, and just laughed.   (page 176)

Although both minimise the danger, they do so differently, Blunden by understating, Graves by trivialising. Blunden is more visual; the whizzbangs gouge and splinter. Graves is more impersonal; his 'about five yards' is less human than 'two or three steps'. Similar contrasts can be seen in other passages. This is Blunden describing bayonet training:

> ... a Scottish expert, accompanied by well-fed, wool-clad gymnastic demonstrators, preached to us the beauty of the bayonet, though I fear his comic tales of Australians muttering 'In, out, – on guard', and similar invocations of 'cold steel' seemed to most of us more disgusting than inspiring in that peacefully ripening farmland.
> (Chapter 9)

Graves is more brutal:

> In bayonet-practice, the men had to make horrible grimaces and utter blood-curdling yells as they charged .... 'Hurt him, now! In at the belly! Tear his guts out!' they would scream, as the men charged the dummies.   (page 195)

Quoting the instructors' orders makes the passage dramatic and closer to showing why bayonet training was disgusting, rather than just telling us it was, as Blunden does. On the other hand, Graves lacks Blunden's contrast with the 'peacefully ripening farmland', part of the pastoral theme which runs throughout *Undertones of War*. With it, Blunden asserts a set of values against those of war much more clearly than Graves does, even though earlier in the chapter from which the above quotation comes (Chapter 21) Graves says he and Sassoon 'defined the war . . . by making contrasted definitions of peace. With Siegfried it was hunting, nature, music, and pastoral scenes; with me, chiefly children' (page 191). How convincing is this claim? Does it partly explain the account Graves gives of his own childhood in *Goodbye to All That*, especially on holiday in Wales and Germany?

Answering questions on *Goodbye to All That*

Questions about *Goodbye to All That* are likely to be either factual or stylistic; they will ask about either what Graves says or how he says it. The factual questions may not necessarily be about the book as history; they may concern Graves's attitudes and opinions. What is his attitude to the war? How does he regard the other members of his family? What is his opinion of formal education? What political views did he develop as he grew older and how seriously did he hold them? All these questions can be answered only on the basis of a good knowledge of the book, which you must read not only with attention to its vivid details but also with awareness of the outlook on life Graves suggests by them and the values they imply.

As an example of a question about what Graves says in *Goodbye to All That*, take 'What is Graves's attitude to the army?' To answer this you will need to have read Chapters 10 to 26 closely, selecting from them illuminating comments and judging Graves's general feelings about the army. Here is a possible answer:

What is Graves's attitude to the army?

Graves's attitude to the army is very far from simple. Although there is much he dislikes and disapproves of about it, he does not reject everything about the army and in some ways he shares the military outlook. He has, in fact, several different ways of evaluating the army.

First, he shows a strong preference for the soldiers in the trenches rather than those who lead them from behind. He is naturally sympathetic with the men who, like him, actually carry out the nasty work of fighting and killing and being killed, and he shares their contempt for staff officers and planners, who order the fighting troops to do impossibly dangerous things. His contempt increases the further away the commanders are from the battlefield; the dugout colonels and generals in London are worse than the staff-officers in France.

Overlying this almost geographical value-system, however, is another based on Graves's regimental pride. For him, the Royal Welch Fusiliers, even those he dislikes personally, are the best soldiers in the army, perhaps in any army; other troops are judged in comparison with them. Such incompetent soldiers as the Public Schools Battalion, who get lost on patrol, or the Highland Light Infantry who panic one night during the battle of Loos, earn Graves's disapproval for their lack of training and discipline. Even the Welsh Regiment, with whom he first serves and whose men have much of his sympathy, is judged adversely in comparison with the Royal Welch Fusiliers. Although the Royal Welch, especially its Second Battalion, is a regiment much given to petty regulations and spiteful discipline, yet as the Surrey-man says to Graves, 'in trenches I'd rather be with this battalion than with any other I have met' (page 107).

This brings up Graves's fundamental ambivalence about the army and war in general. Although he learns to hate the war and makes clear how terrible it was, he maintains a set of values which are quite traditional and based on the military need for courage, discipline and effective training. In Chapter 17 Graves evaluates the fighting qualities of various kinds of troops using quite orthodox military standards. He seems unaware that he is thus giving unconscious approval to the army's own values. The most striking instance of this is his praise of drill in the same chapter, which he justifies to some Canadian troops by saying that 'when they were better at fighting than the Guards they could perhaps afford to neglect their arms-drill' (page 156). Implicit in this is the assumption that being able to fight like the Guards is a good thing.

Surprisingly, then, despite the terrible things which the war did to him, Graves's attitude to the army is not hatred. Indeed, it might be said that what he disapproved of in the army was its failure as a whole to live up to the high military standards Graves found among certain of its fighting men, especially the Royal Welch Fusiliers.

The second type of question concerns style, which has already been considered in Part 3 and in the comparisons with Sassoon and Blunden earlier in this part. In answering these questions you will need the help of notes made while reading the text. Make a record of the many different kinds of writing Graves uses and for what purpose. Note the page references of passages which are striking stylistically, so that you can find them again when you need quotations for an essay or are revising for an examination. Study some passages closely, with the help of the notes in Part 2, paying particular attention to Graves's use of slang, technical language, literary references and factual detail. Note his fondness for short, direct sentences and for dialogue and how he shapes his material into small narratives, often very loosely linked. Consider especially Graves's ways of sounding informal and conversational.

As an example, take the question 'Discuss Graves's use of humour'. Many of the incidents in the book are humorous, although often the humour is mixed with bitterness. To answer the question, you must select a few instances, note their effect and then suggest what the presence of humour in the book adds to its meaning. Here is a possible answer:

Discuss Graves's use of humour.

Robert Graves makes frequent use of humour in *Goodbye to All That*. Sometimes it seems there simply to amuse, as in the story of how he met the Bishop of Liverpool after the latter had been stung by a jellyfish (page 224). More often, however, Graves's humour has a serious purpose, as in the story about his father who, on learning that Robert travelled to school without paying for his rail ticket, went to the station, bought a ticket and tore it up without using it (Chapter 7). This is ridiculous, but it also illustrates his father's moral rectitude.

Most of the humour in *Goodbye to All That* is used to illustrate attitudes and themes. This applies particularly to the war scenes. Graves's account in Chapter 14 of his first meal in the Royal Welch Fusiliers' mess at Laventie is full of farcical incidents: the repeated changes of the gramophone records, the refusal to serve whisky to a 'young' officer of forty-two, the rudeness of the second-in-command to Graves and another new officer. But the humour here is bitter; men facing death in the trenches should not act so stupidly and unpleasantly to each other. Graves includes the scene not just to amuse but also to undermine the notion that all soldiers are heroes and gentlemen.

Graves's humour often turns into irony, especially at the expense of the army as an institution. Its regulations, its orders and its plans usually have unforeseen and unwelcome consequences. Sometimes this is comic, as when Graves's battalion is sent by mistake to Cork instead of York (page 221), but more often the confusion, though described jauntily by Graves, is deadly serious. The stark difference between military expectation and the terrible reality is highlighted by the incident in the Loos attack (Chapter 15), when an officer calls his men cowards for not obeying his order to advance, only to be told by his sergeant that they cannot move because they have all been killed by a machine-gun.

Graves returns to a less brutal humour in the last few chapters of *Goodbye to All That*, but the scenes in Egypt make quite clear that his humour is based on his perception of the absurd. Being a professor of English at a university which has no English books and whose students hardly understand that language is as absurd as being an infantry officer in a trench war whose battalion commander insists he learn to ride a horse.

In general, then, Graves uses humour to reveal absurdity, the gap between pretension and actuality, between what people would like to do or believe and what really happens. By showing this gap appearing in many small instances and in connection with several large institutions or events, Graves makes the whole of his early life seem surrounded by absurdity. The war contributes to this, because its horror and insanity undermine the certainties of pre-war England; repeatedly Graves shows how the civilians at home fail to understand what the fighting is really like, substituting their own fantasy for reality. And for soldiers like him, life in England seems unreal after the terrors of trench warfare. Thus the humour of *Goodbye to All That* contributes to the theme of estrangement in the book.

Part 5

Suggestions for further reading

The text

GRAVES, ROBERT: *Goodbye to All That*, Cassell, London, 1957, and Penguin Books, Harmondsworth, 1960.

This is the edition used in the preparation of these Notes. There are considerable differences between this text, revised by Graves, and the first edition, published by Jonathan Cape, London, 1929.

Other books by Robert Graves

Collected Poems 1975, Cassell, London, 1975. Because Graves has repeatedly revised his poems, rejecting those he dislikes, none of his early war poems are included in this selection.

The Crane Bag, Cassell, London, 1969. A book of short essays, some of them of autobiographical interest and connected with *Goodbye to All That*.

The Shout and Other Stories, Penguin, Harmondsworth, 1968. A collection of short stories, including 'Christmas Time' and 'You Win, Houdini', which are connected with *Goodbye to All That*.

Books about Graves and *Goodbye to All That*

FUSSELL, PAUL: *The Great War and Modern Memory*, Oxford University Press, New York and London, 1975. Chapter 6 contains comments on *Goodbye to All That*, but the whole book is of interest in studying the literary response to the war.

RUTHERFORD, ANDREW: *The Literature of War*, Macmillan, London, 1978. Chapter 4 discusses First World War literature, including Graves's contribution.

SEYMOUR-SMITH, MARTIN: *Robert Graves: His Life and Works*, Hutchinson, London, 1982.

Books about the First World War

ASHWORTH, TONY: *Trench Warfare 1914–1918*, Macmillan, London, 1980.

BLUNDEN, EDMUND: *Undertones of War*, Penguin Books, Harmondsworth, 1937 (and many reprints).

FULLER, J. F. C.: *The Conduct of War 1789–1960*, Eyre & Spottiswoode, London, 1961. This contains chapters setting the First World War in the context of modern military history.

KEEGAN, JOHN: *The Face of Battle*, Jonathan Cape, London, 1976, and Penguin Books, Harmondsworth, 1978. Chapter 4 tries to describe what it was like for the British soldier in the trenches.

REMARQUE, ERICH MARIA: *Im Westen Nichts Neues*, Propylaen, Berlin, 1929; translated by A. W. Wheen as *All Quiet on the Western Front*, Putnam, London, 1929. A famous novel of the First World War by a German author.

SASSOON, SIEGFRIED: *The Complete Memoirs of George Sherston*, Faber & Faber, London, 1937. 'George Sherston' is Sassoon's name for himself; the second part, *Memoirs of an Infantry Officer*, is available separately as a paperback.

SASSOON, SIEGFRIED: *The War Poems*, edited by Rupert Hart-Davis, Faber & Faber, London, 1983.

TAYLOR, A. J. P.: *The First World War: an Illustrated History*, Hamish Hamilton, London, 1963, and Penguin Books, Harmondsworth, 1966. A lively, brief history, with excellent illustrations.

TERRAINE, JOHN: *White Heat: the New Warfare, 1914–18*, Sidgwick & Jackson, London, 1982. The leading British historian of the war describes its technology.

WINTER, DENIS: *Death's Men: Soldiers of the Great War*, Allen Lane, London, 1978. A detailed account of the British soldier in the First World War, mainly drawn from memoirs.

The author of these notes

CHRISTOPHER MACLACHLAN was educated at the University of Edinburgh, and is now a lecturer in English at the University of St Andrews. He has published an article on Dryden and is the author of York Notes on *Selected Poems of Alexander Pope*.

The first 200 titles

		Series number
BEN JONSON	*The Alchemist*	(102)
	Volpone	(15)
RUDYARD KIPLING	*Kim*	(114)
D. H. LAWRENCE	*Sons and Lovers*	(24)
	The Rainbow	(59)
	Women in Love	(143)
CAMARA LAYE	*L'Enfant Noir*	(191)
HARPER LEE	*To Kill a Mocking-Bird*	(125)
LAURIE LEE	*Cider with Rosie*	(186)
THOMAS MANN	*Tonio Kröger*	(168)
CHRISTOPHER MARLOWE	*Doctor Faustus*	(127)
	Edward II	(166)
SOMERSET MAUGHAM	*Of Human Bondage*	(185)
	Selected Short Stories	(38)
HERMAN MELVILLE	*Billy Budd*	(10)
	Moby Dick	(126)
ARTHUR MILLER	*Death of a Salesman*	(32)
	The Crucible	(3)
JOHN MILTON	*Paradise Lost I & II*	(94)
	Paradise Lost IV & IX	(87)
	Selected Poems	(177)
V. S. NAIPAUL	*A House for Mr Biswas*	(180)
SEAN O'CASEY	*Juno and the Paycock*	(112)
	The Shadow of a Gunman	(200)
GABRIEL OKARA	*The Voice*	(157)
EUGENE O'NEILL	*Mourning Becomes Electra*	(130)
GEORGE ORWELL	*Animal Farm*	(37)
	Nineteen Eighty-four	(67)
JOHN OSBORNE	*Look Back in Anger*	(128)
HAROLD PINTER	*The Birthday Party*	(25)
	The Caretaker	(106)
ALEXANDER POPE	*Selected Poems*	(194)
THOMAS PYNCHON	*The Crying of Lot 49*	(148)
SIR WALTER SCOTT	*Ivanhoe*	(58)
	Quentin Durward	(54)
	The Heart of Midlothian	(141)
	Waverley	(122)
PETER SHAFFER	*The Royal Hunt of the Sun*	(170)
WILLIAM SHAKESPEARE	*A Midsummer Night's Dream*	(26)
	Antony and Cleopatra	(82)
	As You Like It	(108)
	Coriolanus	(35)
	Cymbeline	(93)
	Hamlet	(84)
	Henry IV Part I	(83)
	Henry IV Part II	(140)
	Henry V	(40)
	Julius Caesar	(13)
	King Lear	(18)
	Love's Labour's Lost	(72)
	Macbeth	(4)
	Measure for Measure	(33)
	Much Ado About Nothing	(73)